Joyce To "enjoy" in your
new ki❤ Christmas 2000
Love, Linda

Boston Tea Parties

Recipes from the
MUSEUM OF FINE ARTS, BOSTON

MFA PUBLICATIONS
a division of the Museum of Fine Arts, Boston

Revised edition
© 2000 Museum of Fine Arts, Boston
All rights reserved. No part of this book may be repro-
duced or transmitted in any form or by any means
electronic or mechanical, including photography, re-
cording, or any other information storage and retrieval
systems, without prior permission in writing from the
publisher.

Library of Congress Catalog Card Number: 00 132141
ISBN: 0-87846-559-6

Published by MFA Publications
a division of the Museum of Fine Arts, Boston
295 Huntington Avenue
Boston, MA 02115

Additional copies of this book may be ordered from
the Museum Shops, Museum of Fine Arts, Boston
(617) 369-3575   www.mfa.org/shop

Front cover: Mary Cassatt, *The Tea* (detail), 1879–80
Back cover: Dorothy Lake Gregory, *The Mad Teaparty*
Back cover flap: Scott Prior, *Nanny and Rose* (detail),
1983
Page 1: Peter Plamondon, *Quilt with Green Teapot*
(detail), 1975
Page 2: Mary Cassatt, *Afternoon Tea Party*, 1891

Photographs of the works of art are from the Museum
of Fine Arts, Boston
Produced by the Ladies Committee Associates and
funded by the Ladies Committee of the Museum of
Fine Arts, Boston

Copyedited by Patricia Draher
Designed by John Hubbard
Typeset by Pamela Zytnicki
Produced by Marquand Books, Inc., Seattle
Printed and bound by C&C Offset Printing Co., Ltd.,
Hong Kong

Contents

7   Foreword

8   Ingredients and Techniques

14   Tea

24   Petite Sandwiches and Fillings

44   Tea Breads

62   Bar Cookies

84   Drop Cookies

106   Shaped Cookies

136   Cakes

156   Potpourri

179   List of Works of Art

184   Acknowledgments

187   Index

Tea table
Massachusetts (Boston), 1750–75

Foreword

When the Ladies Committee Associates asked for my blessing of their plan to publish a revision of their *Boston Tea Parties* cookbook, my response was an enthusiastic "yes." Having lived most of my life in England, where the custom of serving afternoon tea is so much a part of everyday life, I thought this a wonderful idea.

Fifteen years ago the newly renovated Evans Wing of the Museum of Fine Arts opened, and so did the newly created Ladies Committee Gallery in the former Fenway Foyer. Since its creation, this gallery has been used to carry on our gracious tradition of serving afternoon tea. Properly brewed tea and freshly baked treats are served from a table set with a gleaming silver tea service while background music is provided by local musicians.

During *Art in Bloom,* the annual spring celebration of fine arts and flowers at the Museum, the Ladies Committee Associates serve a most elegant afternoon tea. Many visitors have enjoyed this special occasion tea as well as the tea we serve during the rest of the year. They find this relaxing repast a perfect way to renew their energy before returning to explore more of the Museum's wonders.

Since the serving of tea has become so much a part of the Museum experience, it was a natural extension of this custom to create *Boston Tea Parties.* Though the book has been out of print for several years, we continue to receive many requests for it. Thus, the Associates have created a bigger and better version of this popular book. Within these pages, you will find favorite sweet and savory kitchen secrets from scores of members of the Ladies Committee and the Ladies Committee Associates. The revised edition contains favorite recipes from the original but also many new ones as well as more works of art. We hope that when you peruse these pages, and the accompanying images drawn from the Museum of Fine Arts' collections, your visual and taste sensations will be forever enhanced.

Malcolm Rogers
Ann and Graham Gund Director

The ultimate criterion for choosing each recipe in this book was taste. To ensure truly delectable results, use fresh ingredients of high quality, be very particular in measuring these ingredients, and follow the mixing and baking directions completely. Before starting to bake, read the recipe and directions carefully and then assemble all necessary ingredients and equipment.

Ingredients
and
Techniques

Teapot
Made by DAVID DAVISON, born 1942

Woman cooking
Greece (Tanagra), about 5th century B.C.

Woman grating cheese
Greece (Tanagra), about 5th century B.C.

Ingredients

Successful baking starts with the freshest and finest ingredients, those of high and uniform quality. Each ingredient has a special function and contributes uniquely to the finished product. Use only the ingredients listed in the recipe; any improvisation will alter the results. All ingredients should be at room temperature unless otherwise stated. The following are descriptions of the forms of particular ingredients you should look for as you prepare to bake.

BUTTER: Recipes call for either butter (salted) or unsalted butter. Unsalted butter is richer in flavor because it contains a higher ratio of cream to water. If desired, any solid vegetable shortening may be substituted for butter, with one exception: 1 cup of butter equals ⅞ cup of lard.

SUGAR: Use white, fine granulated sugar. Brown sugar refers to light brown sugar, unless the recipe specifies dark brown sugar. Confectioners' sugar is 10X powdered sugar; it should be sifted before measuring or decorating.

EGGS: Use very fresh *large* grade A eggs, unless otherwise stated.

MILK: Use *whole,* grade A milk.

FLOUR: Use white, all-purpose flour, which is a blend of hard and soft wheat flours; it can be either bleached or unbleached. On occasion, cake flour is specifically called for; it is highly refined flour, milled from soft winter wheat. All flour has a tendency to pack on standing, so always sift flour once before measuring, even if the flour label says "presifted."

BAKING POWDER: Use fresh double-action baking powder that is aluminum free. Fresh baking powder will fizz when added to water.

BAKING SODA: Use very fresh baking soda. Fresh baking soda will fizz when added to vinegar.

COCOA: Use *Dutch processed,* unsweetened cocoa powder. Do not substitute prepared cocoa mix.

CHOCOLATE CHIPS: Always buy *premium-brand* chips. Use semisweet chocolate chips, unless milk chocolate chips or white baking chips are specifically called for.

CHOCOLATE: Use a very high quality dark or white chocolate.

SPICES: Measurements are for ground spices, unless otherwise noted. Store in airtight container to seal in flavor.

VANILLA: Use only *pure* vanilla extract packaged in dark glass bottles. Imitation vanilla contains synthetic vanillin made from wood-pulp by-products and not from vanilla beans.

CITRUS PEEL: Grate lightly to remove only the colored portion of the peel. The pith (white part underneath) tends to be bitter.

OATMEAL: Quick oatmeal is 1-minute rolled oats; old fashioned oatmeal is 5-minute rolled oats. Use both *uncooked*. Quick and old fashioned rolled oats can be used interchangeably, but instant oatmeal cannot be substituted for either kind.

DRIED FRUITS: Dried fruits (apricots, dates, raisins, currants) must be soft and fresh, because baking will not soften them. If they have become too dry, steam them over hot water for a few minutes until they plump; then dry them between layers of paper towels. Do not substitute prepared, chopped, sugared dates.

NUTS: Use freshly shelled nuts. A particular nut may be specified in a recipe, but generally speaking, pecans, walnuts, almonds, and hazelnuts are interchangeable.

Techniques

Use standard measuring cups and spoons that conform to United States Bureau of Standards specifications. Unless otherwise stated in the recipe, all measurements are level. Even a small variation in the amount of an ingredient can change the balance of a recipe enough to cause a poor result.

MEASURE: For *liquid measures*, use a glass cup marked on the side and having a top that extends above the cup line (to prevent spilling). For accuracy, set the cup on a level surface, pour liquid into it, and check the exact amount at eye level.

To measure *dry ingredients*, use nested metal cups available in sets of four (1 cup, ½ cup, ⅓ cup, ¼ cup). These do not have extensions above the cup measure, nor do they have lips. For a level measurement, sift or lightly spoon dry ingredients into the cup, and draw a straight metal spatula across the top. The only exception to this rule is brown sugar; it must be packed into the cup so firmly that it holds the shape of the cup when turned out.

The standard set of measuring spoons includes 1 tablespoon, 1 teaspoon, ½ teaspoon, and ¼ teaspoon. Fill the spoon to level for liquid ingredients; for dry ingredients, fill the spoon to heaping and level off with a straight metal spatula.

Methods of mixing and the order of combining ingredients are important in baking. For example, a basic principle for cookies of all kinds: never work or beat the dough after the flour has been added, as it will make the cookies tough.

PREHEAT: Set the oven at the temperature specified by the recipe and preheat for 15 minutes before baking. *If using a glass pan*, set the oven 25 degrees lower than temperature recommended in recipe.

MELT: Liquefy an ingredient over low heat.

BLEND OR MIX: Combine two or more ingredients so that each loses its identity.

STIR: With an electric mixer on medium-low speed, mix until all the ingredients are just blended. By hand, hold the spoon upright and use a horizontal circular motion.

CREAM: Beat softened butter with an electric mixer or a wooden spoon until smooth and fluffy. Gradually add sugar and continue mixing until the substance is light.

BEAT: With an electric mixer at high speed, briskly blend ingredients over and over to enclose air and make the mixture light. By hand, use a vertical circular motion.

WHIP: Rapidly beat light mixtures, such as egg whites and creams.

FOLD: Combine two prepared mixtures, the lighter one on top of the heavier. Use a rubber spatula to cut down gently through the center of mixtures; lightly lift and fold over the ingredients. Repeat carefully until the mixtures are blended. Do not overmix.

NOTE: *Italicized comments throughout the book provide tips on preparation and presentation that will give your baked goods a special flair.*

A steaming cup of tea quenches the thirst and soothes the spirit. One of life's greatest pleasures is the rich taste of tea that is freshly brewed and shared with friends.

Tea

Teapot with Dutch fittings
Japan, about 1670–1700

ABOVE: Tea bags
Japan, 19th century

Tea jar
Japan, 16th–17th century

OPPOSITE: HONORÉ DAUMIER
Le thé foin (Here you are, sir. I've brought an entire bale, sir.
Make your own tea, as strong as you like.), 1857

History of Tea

Tea is the world's most popular beverage after water. Both green and black tea are made from the same plant—the warm-weather evergreen *Camellia sinensis*. Green tea, quite popular in Asia, is simply the chopped, rolled, and dried leaf. Black tea is made by fermenting dried green tea.

Known in China as *cha*, tea was discovered about 2700 B.C. by the Chinese emperor Shen-Nong. The Dutch East India Company first brought tea to Holland in 1610. For a time, tea was regarded as medicine and, by religious communities, as an aid to meditation. By 1650 it had become popular as a fashionable beverage with the British upper class. A tax of three pence per pound was imposed by the British on tea sold in the American Colonies—thereby giving rise to the historic Boston Tea Party.

Although originally an item restricted to the wealthy, by the second half of the 18th century, tea had become an everyday beverage. Both well-to-do homes and rural farmhouses had the teapot, tea cups, and spoons that made possible the ceremonious social ritual of tea drinking.

Kinds of Tea

Assam

A strong, full-bodied Indian tea with a powerful maltlike flavor and a rich golden color. A major ingredient in the various blends known as English Breakfast tea, Assam is recommended for the early morning.

Ceylon

This tea is golden in color and of medium strength. It is very good iced for a refreshing drink on a hot summer afternoon.

Darjeeling

The best Darjeeling is grown high in the foothills of the Himalayas and makes a light, fragrant tea with a spicy aroma. It also is very good served iced.

Earl Grey

This tea is a blend of black teas, scented with oil of bergamot. It was created for the second Earl Grey of England in the 1830s.

Gunpowder Green

The best known green China tea, so called because its dry leaves were thought to resemble gunpowder. This fragrant, pale tea is particularly low in caffeine.

Jasmine

The dried flowers of the scented white jasmine are added to black or green tea to make this fragrant beverage. It is often served as a digestive after a meal.

OPPOSITE: PIERRE FILLOEUL
Woman Having Tea, 1749

How to Brew the Perfect Pot of Tea

The care with which tea is prepared is as important as the variety of tea selected.

To condition a china or earthenware teapot, rinse it with hot water.

Put 1 teaspoon of tea leaves in the pot for each cup desired, plus one for the pot.

Bring fresh, cold water to a full rolling boil, pour over the tea, and allow to steep covered for 3 to 5 minutes (overbrewing causes a bitter taste). Remove holder or tea ball, if used.

Use a "tea cozy" (padded cover) to keep the tea hot while it is steeping and being served.

Serve tea accompanied with tiny sandwiches, breads, and sweets. Whether the tea menu is simple or elaborate, it should be interesting and distinctive.

Ginger "Tea"

2-inch piece of ginger
4 cups water, preferably spring
Honey or brown sugar

From a piece of fresh, unpeeled ginger cut 8 to 10 coin-shaped slices; place in a medium saucepan. Grate about ½ inch of ginger into the pan with the slices. Cover ginger with water and bring to a boil. Lower heat and simmer for 20 minutes. Add honey or brown sugar to taste and serve.

YIELD: 4 CUPS

This drink is also refreshing served iced.

Russian Tea ·

1 cup water

1 cup sugar

1 stick cinnamon

2 oranges, juiced (reserve rinds)

2 lemons, juiced (reserve rinds)

2 cups pineapple juice

6 cups water

1 cup strong tea

¼ cup dark rum (optional)

Boil 1 cup water, sugar, and cinnamon for 5 minutes. Add orange, lemon, and pineapple juice. Boil orange and lemon rinds in 2 cups of the water for 3 minutes; strain and combine with fruit juice mixture. Add remaining 4 cups water and heat to boiling. Just before serving, add freshly made strong tea and, if desired, rum. Serve hot, garnished with a slice of lime or lemon. Typically served in special glasses.

YIELD: 10 CUPS

The fruit syrup (first three steps) may be prepared ahead and stored in refrigerator.

Tomato Bouillon "Tea" ·

22 cups boiling water

20 beef bouillon cubes

4 cans (46 ounces each) tomato juice

1½ cups sugar

4 sticks cinnamon

3 tablespoons whole cloves

Combine ingredients and simmer about 1 hour.

YIELD: 45 CUPS

OPPOSITE: ALBERT ANDRÉ
Woman at Tea, 1917

RIGHT: Tea caddy
Made by MIURA KENYA, 1821–1889

Classic Chilled Tea ·

8 cups water

8 tea bags

Ice cubes

Sugar (optional)

Lemon and lime slices
   (optional)

In a nonreactive saucepan, bring 4 cups of the water in your recipe to boiling over high heat. Detach tags from tea bags and tie the strings together for easier handling. Remove saucepan from heat, add tea bags, and cover. Steep for 5 minutes; then discard tea bags. Pour remaining 4 cups cold water into a large pitcher and add prepared tea; cover and let stand until ready to serve. Do not refrigerate, or tea will become cloudy. If tea does cloud, gradually add a small amount of boiling water until it clears. Fill pretty goblets with ice cubes and pour tea over. Serve with sugar and thin lemon and lime slices.

YIELD: 8 CUPS

Épergne
Marked by JOHN PARKER AND EDWARD WAKELIN,
active 1762

Iced Tea ·

13 cups water

¾ cup frozen lemonade
    concentrate, thawed

3 sprigs mint

½ cup sugar (scant)

11 tea bags

Bring water to a boil and pour over other ingredients. Let steep 5 minutes. Remove tea bags and mint; refrigerate.

YIELD: 14 CUPS

Fruited Tea Punch · · · · · · · · · · · · · · · · · ·

6 cups water

8 cups sugar

¼ pound black tea

4 cups fresh lemon juice
    (1½ dozen lemons)

1 cup orange juice

1 cup grape juice

⅛ teaspoon cayenne pepper
    (optional)

6 sprigs mint, leaves only, cut
    fine

4 cups strawberries, washed,
    drained, and sliced

2 cups raspberries, washed and
    drained

In saucepan, heat 4 cups of the water and the sugar until sugar is dissolved. Cool sugar syrup. Boil remaining 2 cups water and pour over tea. Steep for 5 minutes; strain, and set aside until cool. Combine sugar syrup, tea, lemon juice, orange juice, grape juice, cayenne pepper, and mint. Refrigerate until ready to serve. Pour punch over ice into a cold punch bowl. Add strawberries and raspberries.

YIELD: 10 TO 12 CUPS

To serve, chill glasses ahead of time and, if desired, dip rims into sugar for a frosted look.

Tea sandwiches should be a feast for the eye as well as the palate—dainty, attractive, and festive. Make these fancy sandwiches extremely thin, all but transparent. Choose garnishes that enhance the flavor of the filling so that your sandwiches will taste as good as they look.

Petite Sandwiches and Fillings

Teapot
Germany (Meissen), about 1730–35

Tea Sandwiches

For tea sandwiches, use thinly sliced bread of firm texture. Day-old bread is best, unless the sandwiches are to be rolled. For rolled pinwheel sandwiches, you need fresh bread. In either case, slice the bread carefully with a long, sharp knife, preferably a serrated blade.

The most important step in preparing these sandwiches is to prevent the fillings from soaking into the bread. To do this, cream softened unsalted butter until it is light and fluffy, and then spread a very thin layer over prepared bread slices before adding the filling.

Spread fillings evenly to the very edge of the bread. Most fillings can be made a day ahead and stored in the refrigerator. Fillings made of uncooked vegetables should be prepared just before serving to avoid loss of vegetable juices and crispness.

When making a large quantity of sandwiches, set up an assembly line for each step—cutting, spreading, garnishing, and storing.

Sandwiches prepared ahead can be stored in the refrigerator in plastic wrap or in a pan lined with a damp cloth and covered with plastic wrap. Many sandwich ingredients are suitable for freezing for a period of 2 to 3 weeks. Those that *do not freeze* well include egg whites (they become rubbery), vegetables and fruits (they lose crispness), and mayonnaise.

Fancy Sandwiches

Canapés

These open-face sandwiches are best assembled just before serving; otherwise, they become soggy. Beautiful canapés begin with clever cutting of assorted breads. Remove all crusts and using cookie cutters create fancy shapes—crescents, rounds, stars, diamonds, etc. Prepare the bread early in the day, wrap tightly, and store at room temperature. Prepare fillings of contrasting flavors, textures, and colors ahead of time and refrigerate, but bring spreads to room temperature before using, so the bread does not tear.

Decorate canapés with edible garnishes like chopped parsley, sliced olives, ground nuts, sieved hard-cooked egg yolks, grated cheeses, thinly sliced vegetables or fruits, capers, caviar, and flowers.

DOROTHY LAKE GREGORY, *The Mad Teaparty*

Closed Sandwiches

To make full-size sandwiches, spread the buttered side of one slice lightly with filling, spreading evenly to the edges. Cover with another buttered slice, and press gently together. Cut the crust from the bread with a sharp knife. Wrap each sandwich in plastic wrap and chill at least 1 hour. Cut each full-size sandwich into four squares, four triangles, or four strips. *Garnish by dipping an edge in mayonnaise or softened unsalted butter and then into minced fresh herbs.*

Pinwheel Sandwiches

Using very fresh bread, remove the crusts from six (or more) slices. Place the slices between waxed paper and gently run a rolling pin over the bread to increase flexibility. Select fillings that will hold pinwheel sandwiches together. Smooth butter or cream cheese mixtures are especially good. Do not attempt to use salad mixtures for this type of sandwich.

First, lightly spread one side of each slice with softened unsalted butter; then cover with a generous amount of filling, leaving a ¼-inch border on all sides. Start at one end of the slice and roll up tightly as a jellyroll. Wrap each roll in plastic wrap and chill for at least 1 hour. Cut in ⅜-inch slices across the rolls and serve. If a garnish is desired, place a row of the selected food end to end, along the starting edge of the roll, which places the garnish in the center of the pinwheel.

Select a garnish appropriate to the primary filling— stuffed olives, small sweet pickles, fresh or canned asparagus spears, cherries, or nasturtiums.

PETER PLAMONDON
Quilt with Green Teapot, 1975

Ribbon Sandwiches

Remove the crusts from two thin slices of dark bread and two thin slices of white bread; trim as necessary, making all slices the same size. Spread one side of each slice lightly with softened unsalted butter. Cover *three* slices with filling (or use various flavored fillings), spreading evenly to the edges of the bread. Stack the three slices like a layer cake, alternating white and dark slices; top with the fourth slice of bread, buttered side down. Press the layers together lightly to make a compact stack. Wrap with plastic wrap and refrigerate for at least 1 hour. Slice the stack into 6 ribbon sandwiches. Cut each ribbon into thirds for a total of 18 finger size sandwiches.

As with pinwheel sandwiches, the filling should be of a type that firms up when chilled and holds the pieces of bread together.

Lavash Sandwiches

These wrapped sandwiches are made using as a base 10-inch or 12-inch round flour tortillas (flavored or plain), sandwich wraps, or large rectangular Armenian flatbreads called lavash. The first step in constructing is to warm the wrapper so that it does not tear. Place in a microwave oven on high heat for 10 to 15 seconds, or wrap in aluminum foil and place in a preheated 350° oven for 3 to 5 minutes. Spread about 1 cup of filling evenly over each wrapper, leaving at least a 1-inch border around the edge. (Be careful not to overstuff the wrap.) Fold the bottom edge of the wrap upward toward the center, and roll the wrapper until it completely encloses the filling. Cover each roll in plastic wrap and store in the refrigerator for up to 4 hours. When they are ready to serve as tea sandwiches, slice each roll with a sharp knife into rounds about 1 inch in length. Arrange on a serving plate cut side down.

If you use round tortillas as the base and if the filling has not reached the outer edge, trim a little off each end.

BARNET RUBENSTEIN
Oyster Pails #4, 1978–79

Butter Spread Sandwiches

Shrimp Butter ·

1 cup butter, softened

1 cup cooked shrimp, minced

¼ teaspoon salt

⅛ teaspoon paprika

1 tablespoon lemon juice

Cream butter thoroughly. Add shrimp, salt, paprika, and lemon juice; mix together. Use as a sandwich filling or canapé spread.

Watercress Butter Roll-ups ·

Watercress, rinsed and dried

½ cup butter, softened

2 teaspoons grated onion

Salt, to taste

12 slices fresh, very thin white
   bread

Remove coarse stems from watercress. Prepare 48 tiny bunches, each about 2 inches in length. Cream butter thoroughly and mix in onion and salt; set aside. Remove bread crusts and cut each slice in half. Spread butter mixture on prepared bread slices. Place 2 watercress bunches at the short ends of each bread slice, overlapping stems in the middle and allowing green leaves to protrude about ½ inch on either side of bread. Roll each slice like a jellyroll. Arrange rolls, seam side down, in a glass pan lined with a damp cloth; cover with another damp cloth. Chill several hours before serving.

Sun-dried Tomato Butter ·

½ cup sun-dried tomatoes, well
   drained

1 cup butter, softened

¼ teaspoon pepper

Between several sheets of paper towel, press any remaining oil or moisture from tomatoes. Mince tomatoes until pieces are small but still have texture. Mix in the butter and pepper; combine well. Spread on toast rounds or use for sandwich filling.

Store sun-dried tomatoes in white wine in a glass container to make them plump and flavorful.

Poppy Seed Butter ·

½ cup butter, softened
½ cup poppy seeds

Cream butter thoroughly. Add poppy seeds and blend. Spread on bread rounds. Serve cold or place rounds under broiler until hot and bubbly.

Savory Butter Pinwheels ·

¼ cup butter, softened
½ cup grated sharp cheese
1 tablespoon mayonnaise
2 tablespoons chopped parsley
1 teaspoon prepared mustard
1 teaspoon Worcestershire
    sauce

Combine butter with the other ingredients to use as a sandwich filling. Follow directions for Pinwheel Sandwiches (page 27). Cut chilled sandwich rolls into thin slices and toast under broiler.

Chive Butter ·

½ cup butter, softened
4 drops Worcestershire sauce
2 tablespoons chopped chives
    or chopped sweet onion

Cream butter thoroughly. Add Worcestershire sauce and chives *or* onion. Spread on bread rounds. Serve cold or place under broiler until hot and bubbly.

Olive Butter ·

½ cup butter, softened
½ teaspoon lemon juice
3 tablespoons chopped olives

Cream butter thoroughly. Combine lemon juice and olives with butter. Spread on bread rounds or use for sandwich filling.

Ginger Butter Triangles

16 thin slices whole wheat
  bread
½ cup butter, softened
2 tablespoons minced
  preserved ginger

Trim crusts from bread. Cream butter thoroughly. Add minced ginger and blend. Spread about 1 tablespoon ginger butter on 8 bread slices; top each with an unbuttered bread slice. Place sandwiches on a jellyroll pan lined with damp towels. Cover sandwiches with damp towels and plastic wrap. Refrigerate until ready to serve. Cut each sandwich diagonally into quarters.

Cinnamon Butter Pinwheels

¼ cup sugar
2 teaspoons cinnamon
⅓ cup butter, softened
12 slices very fresh white bread

Combine sugar and cinnamon; set aside. Cream butter thoroughly. Add cinnamon sugar to butter and beat until light and fluffy. Follow directions for Pinwheel Sandwiches (page 27). Serve sandwiches plain or toast lightly under broiler.

Spiced Pear Butter

1 very ripe *unpeeled* pear
¾ cup unsalted butter,
  softened
2 tablespoons honey
1 teaspoon lemon juice
½ teaspoon cinnamon
¼ teaspoon grated lemon peel
⅛ teaspoon nutmeg

Core pear and cut into 1-inch pieces. Cream butter in food processor. Add pear, a small amount at a time, and process until smooth. Add remaining ingredients and blend well. Spread on bread rounds, or serve with muffins, scones, or toast.

MAURICE BRAZIL PRENDERGAST
Still Life, about 1910–13

Orange Butter

1 cup butter, softened
1 teaspoon grated orange peel
¼ cup orange juice
¼ cup brown sugar, packed

Cream butter thoroughly. Combine with other ingredients and beat until well blended. Spread on bread rounds or on slices of Date Nut Bread (page 48).

Cream Cheese Spread Sandwiches

Cream Cheese and Strawberry Sandwiches

½ teaspoon vanilla
1 teaspoon sugar
8 ounces cream cheese, softened
3 to 4 teaspoons milk
1 small loaf thinly sliced white bread
Fresh strawberries

Add vanilla and sugar to cream cheese. Slowly add enough milk to achieve spreading consistency. Remove crusts from bread and spread cream cheese mixture on each slice. Cut into quarters. Freeze. Shortly before time to serve, remove from freezer and place sliced strawberries on top. Peaches or pears may be substituted.

Raspberry Dainties

3 ounces cream cheese, softened
1 to 2 teaspoons cream
½ cup seedless raspberry jam
¼ cup flaked coconut, toasted

Cut bread into fancy canapé shapes. Combine cream cheese with enough cream to achieve spreading consistency. Spread bread with cream cheese, then jam, and sprinkle with toasted coconut.

Pineapple Cheese Wafers

3 ounces cream cheese,
  softened
3 tablespoons mayonnaise
½ cup chopped pecans
½ cup crushed canned
  pineapple, drained

Blend cream cheese with mayonnaise. Add pecans and crushed pineapple. Spread on crisp crackers or whole wheat bread rounds.

Nut Spread

⅓ cup minced walnuts or
  pecans or pistachios, toasted
6 ounces cream cheese,
  softened
2 to 3 teaspoons milk

Place nuts in a shallow baking pan and toast in a preheated 350° oven for 5 to 10 minutes. Watch carefully and stir often to prevent burning. Set aside. Combine cream cheese with enough milk to achieve spreading consistency. Add nuts; blend well.

Roquefort Spread

3 ounces cream cheese,
  softened
2 ounces Roquefort cheese
1 to 2 tablespoons brandy or
  sherry

Combine cheeses and add enough liquid to achieve spreading consistency.

This spread is excellent served with Pear Bread (see page 52).

Ginger Spread

1 tablespoon cream
8 ounces cream cheese,
  softened
2 tablespoons preserved
  ginger, finely chopped

Add cream to cream cheese to achieve spreading consistency. Blend in chopped ginger.

This spread is delicious served on Date Nut Bread (page 48).

Roasted Red Bell Pepper Canapés ·

1 large red bell pepper

4 ounces cream cheese, softened

1 teaspoon lemon juice

2 to 3 teaspoons extra virgin olive oil

⅛ teaspoon salt

White pepper, to taste

1 teaspoon peeled, grated ginger or to taste

Paprika

Preheat broiler. Place bell pepper in a roasting pan. Char pepper under broiler until blackened on all sides; turn occasionally until pepper collapses, about 10 to 20 minutes. Place in a paper bag and let stand 10 minutes to steam. Let cool; peel, seed, and mince pepper. Combine cream cheese with lemon juice. Thin with enough olive oil to achieve spreading consistency. Add salt, white pepper, and grated ginger. Gently fold in the minced pepper. Spread on bread cut in canapé shapes and garnish with paprika.

Mediterranean Sandwich Wraps ·

2 large red bell peppers, roasted and minced

8 ounces cream cheese, softened

2 teaspoons lemon juice

2 tablespoons extra virgin olive oil

¼ teaspoon white pepper

½ cup crumbled feta cheese

1 jar capers (3 to 4 ounces), drained

2 lavash rectangles

Prepare charred peppers according to the instructions in Roasted Red Bell Pepper Canapés (this page). Combine cream cheese with lemon juice and olive oil; blend well. Add white pepper, feta cheese, and the minced peppers. Follow directions for Lavash Sandwiches (page 29). Divide mixture between the wraps and spread as directed. Arrange capers along the bottom edge of wraps; roll upward so that capers are in the center of the wrap. Place each roll in plastic wrap; store in the refrigerator for several hours. Cut the chilled rolls into 1-inch rounds and serve.

Fish plate

PAINTER RELATED TO THE D'AGOSTINO PAINTER, 350–325 B.C.

Smoked Salmon Lavash Sandwiches · · · · · · · · · · · · ·

4 lavash rectangles or flour
   tortillas (10 inch or 12 inch)
8 ounces cream cheese,
   softened
4 tablespoons capers, drained
2 tablespoons prepared
   horseradish
¼ teaspoon white pepper
2 cups smoked salmon, cut
   into thin strips
1 cup peeled, seeded, and
   chopped cucumber
½ cup chopped fresh dill
3 teaspoons extra virgin
   olive oil

Follow directions for Lavash Sandwiches (page 29).
Combine the cream cheese, capers, horseradish, and
pepper in a small bowl. Divide cream cheese mixture
among the wraps and spread evenly. Mix remaining
ingredients and divide evenly among the wraps. Cut
the chilled rolls into 1-inch rounds.

Salmon Dill Rounds · · · · · · · · · · · · · · · · · · ·

12 slices pumpernickel bread
3 ounces cream cheese,
   softened
2 teaspoons milk
1 teaspoon minced fresh dill
   or ¼ teaspoon dried
¼ cup smoked salmon,
   chopped

Using a biscuit cutter, cut 24 bread rounds. Blend
cream cheese, milk, and dill. Spread each bread round
with a teaspoon of cream cheese mixture. Top each
round with ½ teaspoon salmon. Place sandwiches on a
pan lined with a damp cloth. Cover with plastic wrap
and refrigerate until ready to serve.

Watercress Canapés · · · · · · · · · · · · · · · · · · ·

4 ounces cream cheese,
   softened
1 teaspoon horseradish
⅛ teaspoon salt
Minced watercress

Beat cream cheese until smooth. Add horseradish
and salt. Stir in watercress. Spread on bread cut in
canapé shapes.

Spinach Pimiento Roll-ups

3 lavash rectangles
8 ounces cream cheese, softened
10 ounces box frozen chopped spinach, cooked and squeezed dry
1 jar pimientos (4 ounces), drained and diced
Salt

Follow directions for lavash sandwiches (page 29). Spread a third of the cream cheese on each lavash wrap. Divide spinach and place on top of cream cheese; follow with pimiento on top. Sprinkle each lightly with salt. Roll up tightly and place in plastic wrap. Refrigerate for several hours before cutting into 1-inch rounds.

Date Bacon Sandwiches

4 ounces cream cheese
⅓ cup pitted dates, finely chopped
5 slices bacon, cooked crisp and crumbled
12 slices pumpernickel bread

Beat cream cheese until light; mix in dates and bacon. Spread mixture on 6 of the bread slices, top with remaining slices, and press together gently. Remove crusts and quarter each sandwich diagonally.

Chicken Salad with Cranberry Chutney

1 pound poached chicken breast, shredded
6 ounces cream cheese, softened
⅔ cup Cranberry Chutney (see page 163)
1 teaspoon grated orange peel
2 loaves thinly sliced white or whole wheat bread

Fold together chicken, cream cheese, chutney, and orange peel. Spread thinly as sandwich filling. Remove crusts and cut into desired shapes.

Mayonnaise Spread Sandwiches

Bacon Filling ·

7 slices bacon, cooked crisp
   and chopped

1 pimiento, chopped

¼ cup mayonnaise

Combine all ingredients. Use as a spread or sandwich filling.

Ham Salad Filling · · · · · · · · · · · · · · · · ·

1 cup ground cooked ham

1 hard-cooked egg, finely
   chopped

3 sweet pickles, chopped

1 ounce pimiento, chopped

1 tablespoon green pepper,
   chopped

1 tablespoon sugar

2 tablespoons cider vinegar

⅓ cup mayonnaise

Combine ground ham with egg, pickles, pimiento, and green pepper; set aside. Combine sugar, vinegar, and mayonnaise; blend well. Mix with chopped ingredients.

Crabmeat Filling · · · · · · · · · · · · · · · · ·

6 ounces crabmeat

2 tablespoons celery, finely
   chopped

1 teaspoon curry powder

Mayonnaise

Shred crabmeat and discard all tough spines. Mix crabmeat, celery, and curry powder with enough mayonnaise to moisten.

Chicken Pecan Sandwiches ·

½ cup pecans

4 slices bacon, cooked crisp
and crumbled

2 cups finely chopped cooked
chicken breasts

3 tablespoons snipped chives

4 to 5 tablespoons mayonnaise

Salt and pepper, to taste

2 ounces cream cheese,
softened

¼ cup butter, softened

12 slices white or whole wheat
sandwich bread

Place pecans in a shallow baking pan and toast in a preheated 350° oven for 5 to 10 minutes; watch carefully and stir to prevent burning. Chop pecans coarsely and combine with bacon and chicken. Add chives; stir to mix. Add mayonnaise a little at a time, using just enough to bind the mixture. Season to taste with salt and pepper and set aside. Mix cream cheese and butter until smooth and soft; spread lightly on bread slices. Add chicken filling, dividing evenly among six sandwiches. Follow directions for Closed Sandwiches (page 27).

Watercress Ham Sandwiches ·

8 thin slices white bread

Butter, softened

½ cup minced watercress

¼ cup minced ham

2 tablespoons mayonnaise

Follow directions for Ribbon Sandwiches (page 29). Spread one side of each slice with butter. Combine watercress, ham, and mayonnaise; spread mixture on 6 buttered slices. Stack 3 of the slices, watercress side up; top with a bread slice, buttered side down. Repeat to make second stack. Wrap and refrigerate each stack as directed. To serve, cut each stack into 6 pieces, and then cut each piece crosswise in half.

Broccoli Tea Sandwiches ·

1 cup mayonnaise

2 cups fresh broccoli
  flowerettes, finely chopped

2 tablespoons minced scallions

1 loaf thinly sliced whole wheat
  bread

Combine mayonnaise, broccoli, and scallions. Follow directions for Closed Sandwiches (page 27). Cut into quarters or attractive shapes.

Cucumber Mint Filling ·

¼ cup mayonnaise

Thin slices cucumber

2 teaspoons finely chopped
  fresh mint leaves

Spread bread rounds with mayonnaise. Place a slice of cucumber on each round and garnish with small amount of mint.

Carrot Raisin Filling ·

2 carrots, grated

¼ cup raisins, chopped

½ cup peanut butter

Mayonnaise

Combine carrots, raisins, and peanut butter. Add enough mayonnaise to moisten. Follow directions for Closed Sandwiches (page 27).

English Spread ·

1 cup mayonnaise

1 cup grated Parmesan cheese

1 clove garlic, pressed

1 can artichoke hearts
  (14 ounces), chopped

Mix together all ingredients. Warm over low heat. Serve on crackers or toast rounds.

An aromatic assortment of sweet and
savory breads, thinly sliced, creates a
wonderful addition to the tea table. These
"quick breads" employ fast-acting leavening agents—baking powder and sometimes
baking soda—and are very easy to make.
To ensure a tender loaf, thoroughly combine shortening, egg, and liquid, and then
add the sifted dry ingredients stirring only
enough to moisten the flour.

Tea Breads

ABOVE: Tea kettle
France (Sèvres), 1779

OVERLEAF: SUZUKI HARUNOBU
Ofuji Visits Osen at the Kagiya Teashop, 1769–70

Tea Lime Bread

1 tea bag

½ cup boiling water or less

2 eggs

⅔ cup sugar

½ cup butter, melted

Grated peel of 2 limes

¾ cup unblanched almonds,
    finely chopped

1⅓ cups sifted cake flour

1 teaspoon baking powder

¼ teaspoon baking soda

¼ teaspoon salt

Place tea bag in a 1-cup glass measure; add boiling water to measure ½ cup. Steep until lukewarm; squeeze and discard tea bag. Set aside. Beat eggs until frothy, add sugar, and mix well. Slowly add hot, melted butter and continue beating until thoroughly blended. Add lime peel, almonds, and the tea. Sift flour with baking powder, baking soda, and salt; add to the egg and sugar mixture, blending until just moistened. Pour batter into a greased and floured 9 × 5 × 3-inch loaf pan. Bake on center rack in a preheated 325° oven for 40 to 45 minutes, or until a tester inserted in the center comes out clean. Cool on a wire rack for 15 minutes before removing from pan.

YIELD: 1 LOAF

Jasmine Tea Bread

½ cup strong jasmine tea

¼ cup unsalted butter,
    softened

¾ cup sugar

1 egg

1 tablespoon grated
    orange peel

1 tablespoon grated
    lemon peel

3 cups flour

1 teaspoon baking powder

1 teaspoon baking soda

½ teaspoon salt

¼ teaspoon cinnamon

¾ cup orange juice

Prepare jasmine tea; set aside until cool. Cream butter and sugar together until light. Add lightly beaten egg, orange peel, and lemon peel; beat until well blended. Sift flour with baking powder, baking soda, salt, and cinnamon. Combine orange juice with jasmine tea. Alternately add dry ingredients and liquids to the sugar and butter mixture; blend batter to incorporate ingredients after each addition. Pour into a well greased 9 × 5 × 3-inch loaf pan; let stand for 20 minutes. Bake in a preheated 350° oven for 45 to 55 minutes, or until a tester inserted in the center comes out clean. Cool on a wire rack for 10 minutes before removing from pan.

YIELD: 1 LOAF

English Tea Gingerbread

3 cups flour

2½ teaspoons ginger

1 teaspoon cardamom

1 teaspoon baking soda

⅔ cup currants

⅔ cup coarsely chopped
   blanched almonds

½ cup unsalted butter

½ cup molasses

½ cup light corn syrup

⅓ cup sugar

⅓ cup milk

1 egg

Into a large mixing bowl, sift together flour, ginger, cardamom, and baking soda. Add currants and almonds; mix well and set aside. In a saucepan, combine butter, molasses, corn syrup, and sugar. Over low heat, stir mixture until butter is melted and sugar is dissolved; cool. Using a wooden spoon, stir the cooled mixture and milk into the flour mixture. Beat in egg until all ingredients are well incorporated. Spread batter in a greased 9 × 2-inch round pan, lined on the bottom with greased waxed paper. Bake in a preheated 375° oven for 35 to 45 minutes, or until a tester inserted in the center comes out clean. Do not underbake. Let stand in pan for 10 minutes; turn gingerbread out onto a rack and remove paper.

YIELD: 1 LOAF

*In England, this gingerbread is
served warm with butter.*

Date Nut Bread

1 cup pitted dates, diced

¾ cup dark seedless raisins

¼ cup golden seedless raisins

1 teaspoon baking soda

1 cup boiling water

½ cup butter, softened

1 cup sugar

1 teaspoon vanilla

1 egg

1⅓ cups flour

¾ cup walnuts, coarsely
   chopped

Place dates and raisins in a bowl. Dissolve baking soda in boiling water and pour over the dried fruit. Cream butter and sugar until light and fluffy. Beat in vanilla and egg. Add flour and mix well. Stir in the fruit mixture; add walnuts. Pour the batter into a greased and floured 9 × 5 × 3-inch loaf pan that has been lined on the bottom with greased waxed paper. Bake in a preheated 350° oven for 60 to 70 minutes, or until the bread is dark brown and a tester inserted in the center comes out clean. Let cool for 5 minutes. Invert onto a rack and remove paper. Cool thoroughly before slicing.

YIELD: 1 LOAF

MIRIAM SCHAPIRO
Welcome to Our Home, 1983

Spiced Apple Bread ·

2⅔ cups flour

1 teaspoon baking powder

1 teaspoon baking soda

½ teaspoon salt

2 teaspoons cinnamon

¼ teaspoon ginger

¼ teaspoon nutmeg

3 tablespoons unsalted butter, softened

⅔ cup brown sugar, packed

2 eggs, lightly beaten

1 cup buttermilk

½ cup chopped pecans

1 apple, peeled and chopped

Sift together flour, baking powder, baking soda, salt, cinnamon, ginger, and nutmeg; set aside. Cream butter, sugar, and eggs. Stir in buttermilk, combining mixture thoroughly. Add the dry ingredients, pecans, and apple; stir until moistened. Pour batter into *two* greased 7 × 3 × 2-inch loaf pans. Bake in a preheated 350° oven for 45 to 50 minutes, or until a tester inserted in the center comes out clean. Cool on rack for 10 minutes before removing from pans. Best served warm. To store, cool for 2 hours before wrapping.

YIELD: 2 MEDIUM LOAVES

Pumpkin Bread ·

⅔ cup butter, softened

2⅔ cups sugar

4 eggs

1¾ cups canned pumpkin

⅔ cup orange juice

3½ cups flour

½ teaspoon baking powder

2 teaspoons baking soda

1½ teaspoons salt

1 teaspoon cinnamon

1 teaspoon cloves

⅔ cup chopped nuts

⅔ cup raisins

Cream butter and sugar well, until light. Add eggs, one at a time. Add pumpkin and juice; blend well. Sift together flour, baking powder, baking soda, salt, cinnamon, and cloves; add to batter, mixing until just moistened. Gently fold in nuts and raisins. Pour batter into *two* greased 9 × 5 × 3-inch loaf pans. Bake in a preheated 350° oven for 65 to 75 minutes, or until a tester inserted in the center comes out clean. Cool for 10 minutes before removing from pan. Cool thoroughly before slicing.

YIELD: 2 LOAVES

Irresistible Banana Bread · · · · · · · · · · · · · · · · · · ·

½ cup raisins

⅓ cup dark rum

½ cup unsalted butter, softened

½ cup brown sugar, packed

1 egg

2 teaspoons vanilla

2 cups flour

1 teaspoon baking powder

½ teaspoon baking soda

½ teaspoon salt

1 teaspoon nutmeg

1 teaspoon ginger

3 very ripe bananas, mashed

⅔ cup walnuts, coarsely chopped

½ cup flaked coconut

Place raisins and rum together in a small saucepan. Bring to a boil, lower heat, and simmer 10 minutes. Set aside to cool. Cream butter and sugar; add egg and beat until light and fluffy. Beat in the vanilla. Sift together flour, baking powder, baking soda, salt, nutmeg, and ginger. Add dry ingredients to the creamed mixture alternately with the mashed bananas, stirring well after each addition. Gently fold in the nuts, coconut, and the raisins with rum. Pour evenly into a greased and floured 9 × 5 × 3-inch loaf pan. Bake in a preheated 350° oven for about 1 hour, or until a tester inserted in the center comes out clean. Cool in the pan for 30 minutes; invert onto a wire rack to cool completely. Wrap in plastic wrap and refrigerate overnight before cutting and serving.

YIELD: 1 LOAF

Zucchini Bread ·

2 cups coarsely grated zucchini

3 eggs

2 cups sugar

1 cup vegetable oil

1 tablespoon vanilla

2 cups flour

¼ teaspoon baking powder

2 teaspoons baking soda

1 teaspoon salt

1 tablespoon cinnamon

1 cup nuts, broken

Sprinkle zucchini with salt in colander. Weight with plate and let drain 1 hour. Squeeze out excess moisture. Beat eggs until frothy. Add sugar, oil, and vanilla; beat until thick and pale yellow. Sift together flour, baking powder, baking soda, salt, and cinnamon. Stir zucchini into egg mixture; add dry ingredients. Fold in nuts. Pour into *two* greased and floured 9 × 5 × 3-inch loaf pans. Bake in a preheated 350° oven for 45 to 60 minutes, or until a tester inserted in the center comes out clean. Cool for 10 minutes before removing from pan. Cool thoroughly before slicing.

YIELD: 2 LOAVES

Pear Bread

½ cup unsalted butter,
    softened

1 cup sugar

2 eggs

1 teaspoon vanilla

2 cups flour

1 teaspoon baking powder

½ teaspoon baking soda

½ teaspoon salt

⅛ teaspoon nutmeg

¼ cup buttermilk

1 cup coarsely chopped
    peeled pears

½ cup chopped nuts
    (optional)

Cream butter, add sugar, and beat until light and fluffy. Add eggs and vanilla and beat well. Sift together flour, baking powder, baking soda, salt, and nutmeg; add to butter and sugar mixture alternately with buttermilk. Do not overmix. Gently fold in pears and, if desired, nuts. Pour into a well greased 9 × 5 × 3-inch loaf pan. Bake in a preheated 350° oven for 50 to 60 minutes.

YIELD: 1 LOAF

Bosc, the ultimate baking pear, gives a flavorful result. This loaf stays moist for days.

Apricot Nut Bread

1 cup dried apricots

1 cup sugar

2 tablespoons butter, melted

1 egg

2 cups flour

1 teaspoon baking powder

¼ teaspoon baking soda

1 teaspoon salt

¼ cup water

½ cup orange juice

½ cup chopped walnuts

Cover apricots with warm water and soak for 30 minutes. Drain and cut into small pieces. Cream together sugar, butter, and egg. Sift together flour, baking powder, baking soda, and salt; add dry ingredients alternately to creamed mixture with water and orange juice. Mix only until dry ingredients are moistened. Fold in apricots and walnuts. Pour batter into a greased and floured 9 × 5 × 3-inch loaf pan. Bake in a preheated 350° oven for 55 to 60 minutes. Cool in pan.

YIELD: 1 LOAF

LUIS MELÉNDEZ
Still Life with Melons and Pears, about 1770

Cranberry Lemon Bread

2 cups flour
1 teaspoon baking powder
1 teaspoon baking soda
1 teaspoon salt
¼ cup unsalted butter, softened
1¼ cups sugar
2 eggs, lightly beaten
½ cup buttermilk
½ teaspoon vanilla
1 tablespoon grated lemon peel
1 cup fresh cranberries

Sift together flour, baking powder, baking soda, and salt; set aside. Cream butter and sugar; add eggs and beat well. Stir in buttermilk, vanilla, and lemon peel; combine well. Add dry ingredients; mix just until moistened. Fold in cranberries. Pour batter into a greased 9 × 5 × 3-inch loaf pan. Bake in a preheated 350° oven for 60 minutes, or until a tester inserted in the center comes out clean. Cool in the pan on rack for 10 minutes. Loosen edges with a knife, and remove from pan. Best served warm. To store, cool for 2 hours and wrap well in foil.

YIELD: 1 LOAF

Blueberry Muffins

2 cups flour
1 tablespoon baking powder
½ teaspoon salt
½ cup unsalted butter
1 cup sugar
2 eggs
1 cup milk
1 cup blueberries (fresh or unthawed frozen)
Sugar

Sift together flour, baking powder, and salt; set aside. Cream butter and sugar until light and fluffy. Beat in eggs. Add dry ingredients to creamed mixture alternately with milk; stir to combine after each addition. Carefully fold in blueberries. Fill well greased muffin tins two-thirds full. Sprinkle tops with sugar. In a preheated 400° oven, bake large muffins for 18 to 20 minutes or mini-muffins for about 15 minutes. Remove from tins while warm.

YIELD: 1½ DOZEN LARGE OR 4 DOZEN MINIATURE

If you use unthawed frozen blueberries, quickly coat them with 2 teaspoons of flour to prevent the berries from sinking to the bottom of the muffins.

Rosemary Walnut Muffins ·

2 cups flour

1 tablespoon sugar

2½ teaspoons baking powder

¼ teaspoon salt

1 cup grated Parmesan cheese

3 ounces cream cheese

3 tablespoons dried rosemary
   leaves, crushed

¼ cup chopped walnuts

1 cup milk

1 egg

⅓ cup melted butter, cooled

In a large bowl, sift together flour, sugar, baking powder, and salt. Stir in Parmesan cheese. Cut in cream cheese until mixture resembles coarse meal. Blend in rosemary and walnuts. Mix together milk, egg, and melted butter; add all at once to dry ingredients and stir only to moisten. Fill well greased mini-muffin tins two-thirds full. Bake in a preheated 400° oven for 15 minutes. Remove from tins while warm.

YIELD: 4 DOZEN MINIATURE

Refrigerator Bran Muffins ·

5 cups flour

5 teaspoons baking soda

2 teaspoons salt

2½ cups sugar

8 cups raisin bran cereal

1 cup vegetable oil

4 eggs, beaten

4 cups buttermilk

Sift together flour, baking soda, and salt into large mixing bowl. Blend sugar and cereal with other dry ingredients. Add oil, eggs, and buttermilk; mix well. Fill greased muffin tins two-thirds full. Bake in a preheated 400° oven 15 to 20 minutes. Remove from tins while warm.

YIELD: 4 TO 5 DOZEN

Store the batter in a covered container and keep in the refrigerator up to 6 weeks. Muffins can be baked fresh, as desired.

Scones and Biscuits

Scones and biscuits contain larger amounts of shortening than breads and muffins do. Butter should be cut into flour and other dry ingredients in the same manner as for pastry, and cold liquids added quickly and lightly. Avoid mixing too much, or the texture will be tough rather than light and flaky.

Curry Scones with Chutney Butter ·

4 cups flour

2 tablespoons baking powder

1 teaspoon salt

2 teaspoons curry powder

½ cup cold butter

2 cups finely grated cheddar cheese

1 cup milk

½ cup heavy cream

CHUTNEY BUTTER

½ cup butter, softened

6 tablespoons Major Grey's Chutney

In a large bowl, sift together flour, baking powder, salt, and curry powder. Cut in cold butter until mixture resembles coarse meal. Stir in cheddar cheese with a fork. Add milk and cream; stir lightly to combine. Turn dough out onto a floured surface, knead about 30 seconds, and pat it gently to ¾-inch thickness. Cut into 2-inch rounds and arrange scones on a baking sheet lightly greased or lined with parchment paper. Bake in the middle of a preheated 400° oven for about 12 minutes.

To make chutney butter, combine softened butter and chutney in food processor until well blended.

YIELD: 3 DOZEN

Painted shroud
Egypt, 18th Dynasty, 1570–1293 B.C.

Tiny Tea Biscuits ·

2 cups flour

1 tablespoon baking powder

1 teaspoon salt

¼ cup butter

¼ cup sugar

½ cup raisins

1 egg

⅓–½ cup milk

Egg or milk, for glaze

Sugar

Sift together flour, baking powder, and salt; cut in the butter until mixture resembles coarse meal. Add sugar, raisins, egg, and enough milk to make a soft dough. Mix lightly with a few strokes. Handle the dough quickly and as little as possible. Turn out on a floured surface, knead gently ½ minute, roll to ½-inch thickness, and cut into triangle or diamond shapes. Place on a lightly greased sheet, brush with egg *or* milk, and sprinkle with sugar. Bake in a preheated 450° oven for 12 to 15 minutes.

YIELD: 2 DOZEN

ABOVE: Teapot
England (London), about 1690

OPPOSITE: Cylinda Line teapot, coffeepot,
sugar bowl, and creamer
Designed by ARNE JACOBSEN, 1902–1971

Buttermilk Scones

3¼ cups flour

1 tablespoon baking powder

½ teaspoon baking soda

1 teaspoon salt

3 tablespoons sugar

1 tablespoon grated
   orange peel

½ cup unsalted butter

1 cup currants

1 egg

1¼ cups buttermilk

1 teaspoon vanilla

GRAND MARNIER GLAZE

1 cup confectioners' sugar

2 tablespoons Grand Marnier

2 tablespoons water

In a large bowl, sift together flour, baking powder, baking soda, salt, and sugar. Add orange peel and mix. Cut in butter until mixture resembles coarse crumbs; add currants and set aside. In another bowl, beat egg lightly with a fork; stir in buttermilk and vanilla. Add liquids to dry ingredients; stir just until blended and dough comes together. Scrape dough onto a well-floured surface. Dough will be soft; with a scraper, turn and pat dough gently several times, until a rough ball comes together. Shape into a rectangle that is ¾-inch thick. Using a long knife with a sharp, straight blade, cut dough into diamonds or triangles of equal size. Carefully lift scones onto a lightly greased baking sheet. Bake in a preheated 400° oven for 15 to 18 minutes, or until scones are golden and firm to the touch. Remove scones from baking sheet; transfer to a rack and cool.

To make glaze, warm sugar, Grand Marnier, and water in a small saucepan over medium heat; stir until sugar dissolves and glaze forms. Set rack of scones on a rimmed baking sheet. Drizzle warm glaze over scones; let stand for 5 minutes, or until glaze sets.

YIELD: 3 DOZEN

Buttermilk has an appealing aroma. It adds moistness and promotes browning so that baked goods develop a natural, golden tan.

Butterhorns

PASTRY

1 cup unsalted butter, softened

1½ cups small curd cottage
    cheese

2 cups flour

Salt, to taste

FILLING

½ cup seedless raspberry or
    apricot jam

½ cup walnuts, finely chopped

TOPPING

3 tablespoons unsalted butter,
    melted

¼ cup sugar

2 teaspoons cinnamon

To make the pastry, cream butter and cottage cheese in a large mixing bowl. Add flour and salt. With your hands, divide dough into three equal parts; wrap each in plastic wrap and refrigerate 4 hours or overnight. Roll one ball of dough at a time on a floured surface, making a circle about 10 inches in diameter and ⅛-inch thick. Cut circle into 8 equal wedges using a pastry or pizza cutter.

Combine the jam and nuts for the filling. Spread a thin layer on each wedge. Roll into butterhorns, starting the roll at the wide end and rolling tightly to the point.

For the topping, brush each butterhorn with melted butter. Combine sugar and cinnamon; sprinkle generously over each pastry. Place butterhorns on a greased baking sheet with the pointed ends down. Bake in a preheated 350° oven for 30 to 35 minutes, or until golden brown.

YIELD: 2 DOZEN

Cottage cheese is the surprise ingredient that makes these pastries tender and rich.

Bar cookies, always a favorite, provide
simple pleasures whether prepared plain
or dressed up with fruits, liqueurs, and
fillings. Each bar brings a new look to a
tray of delectable treats. Stir the dry ingredients only until moistened; otherwise, the
cookies will develop a tough texture and
crusty tops. Use the recommended pan
size. After baking, cut the bars into dif-
ferent shapes with a very sharp knife or a
large pizza cutter.

Bar Cookies

Teapot
Germany (Hoechst), about 1750

Thin Chocolate Squares ·

½ cup butter, softened

1 cup brown sugar, packed

2 eggs, beaten

2 ounces unsweetened
   chocolate, melted

1 teaspoon vanilla

½ cup flour

1 cup chopped nuts

Confectioners' sugar

Cream butter and sugar. Add beaten eggs, chocolate, vanilla, flour, and nuts. Spread the batter evenly on a greased and floured 15 × 10-inch jellyroll pan. Bake in a preheated 325° oven for 10 to 12 minutes. Sprinkle the top with confectioners' sugar while still warm; cut into squares.

YIELD: 5 DOZEN

A simple way to line a pan with heavy-duty foil is to turn the pan upside down, tear a piece of foil slightly larger than the pan, and mold it to the outside. Next, remove the foil from the outside of the pan, turn the pan right side up, and insert the formed foil. You can then use the excess foil to lift the whole cake from the pan before cutting it into bars. This method is excellent for any firm bar cookie.

Jon Vie Brownies ·

2 cups sugar

1 cup brown sugar, packed

⅔ cup light corn syrup

1 cup butter, softened

6 eggs

6 ounces unsweetened
    chocolate, melted

2 cups flour

2 cups pecans, chopped

Beat together the sugars, corn syrup, and butter. Mix in eggs, one at a time, just until absorbed. Stir in chocolate. Add flour; stir until blended. Reserve ½ cup of the nuts and stir in the rest. Pour into an *ungreased* 15 × 10 × 2-inch pan; sprinkle remaining ½ cup pecans on top. Bake in a preheated 350° oven for 40 minutes, or until a tester inserted in the center comes out clean. Cool; cut into bars.

YIELD: 5 DOZEN

This recipe is from a famous delicatessen that "vied" to be the best.

Espresso Brownies ·

8 ounces unsweetened
    chocolate

1 cup butter

5 *extra large* eggs

1 tablespoon vanilla

1 drop almond extract

1 teaspoon salt

3 tablespoons instant
    espresso powder

3¾ cups sugar

1⅔ cups flour

3 cups walnut halves

Place chocolate and butter in top of a double boiler over hot water; keep heat low and stir frequently until mixture is melted and smooth. In a large bowl, beat eggs with vanilla, almond extract, salt, espresso powder, and sugar; continue beating at high speed for 10 minutes. On low speed, add chocolate mixture and blend only to combine. Add flour; stir just until moistened. Stir in walnuts. Spoon batter into a 13 × 9 × 2-inch pan lined with lightly greased heavy-duty foil. Smooth top of batter. Bake in a preheated 400° oven for 35 minutes. Cool brownies; refrigerate for 8 hours or overnight. Cut with a serrated knife.

YIELD: 4 DOZEN

OPPOSITE: ROBERT LOUIS FRANK
Coffee Shop, Railway Station—Indianapolis, about 1956; printed 1979

Grand Marnier Brownies ·

BROWNIES

1 ounce unsweetened
   chocolate

1 cup chocolate chips

7½ tablespoons unsalted
   butter

⅔ cup flour

¼ teaspoon baking soda

¼ teaspoon salt

2 eggs

⅔ cup sugar

2 tablespoons Grand Marnier

1 teaspoon vanilla

1 tablespoon grated orange
   peel

¾ cup ground almonds

FROSTING

6 tablespoons unsalted butter,
   softened

2 teaspoons Grand Marnier

1 teaspoon grated orange peel

1 cup confectioners' sugar

GLAZE

¼ cup unsalted butter

⅓ cup chocolate chips

Melt chocolate, chocolate chips, and butter in top of double boiler over simmering water; stir frequently until mixture is melted and smooth. Sift together flour, baking soda, and salt; set aside. In a large mixing bowl, beat eggs until light in color; gradually add sugar. Beat in Grand Marnier, vanilla, and orange peel. Stir in the chocolate mixture until well blended. Fold in the dry ingredients and almonds. Spread batter in a 9 × 9 × 2-inch pan lined with greased foil. Bake in a preheated 325° oven for 22 minutes. Allow brownies to cool in pan before frosting.

For the frosting, beat butter, Grand Marnier, and orange peel together. Add confectioners' sugar and beat until fluffy. Spread frosting over cooled brownies.

To make glaze, combine butter and chocolate chips in top of double boiler over low heat. Stir until melted and well blended. Gently pour warm glaze over frosted brownies and spread evenly, tilting pan to cover all the frosted area. Chill brownies overnight. Remove from pan by lifting foil. Carefully remove foil, and cut brownies with a sharp knife dipped in hot water. Keep refrigerated or freeze.

YIELD: 3 DOZEN

Chocolate Peppermint Squares ·

COOKIES

2 ounces unsweetened
   chocolate

½ cup butter

2 eggs, beaten

1 cup sugar

¼ teaspoon peppermint
   extract

Salt, to taste

½ cup flour

½ cup chopped walnuts

PEPPERMINT FROSTING

2 tablespoons butter, softened

1 cup confectioners' sugar

1 tablespoon cream

¾ teaspoon peppermint
   extract

GLAZE

1 ounce unsweetened
   chocolate

1 tablespoon butter

Melt chocolate and butter over hot water; set aside. Cream together eggs, sugar, peppermint extract, and salt. Add chocolate mixture. Stir in flour and nuts. Pour into a greased 9 × 9 × 2-inch pan. Bake in a preheated 350° oven for 20 to 25 minutes. Cool.

Mix frosting ingredients until smooth. Frost cooled cookies; refrigerate until chilled and set.

To make glaze, melt chocolate and butter together. Drizzle over frosted cookies, tilting pan until glaze covers all. Refrigerate 5 minutes to firm glaze. Cut into squares.

YIELD: 3 DOZEN

It is hard to improve a chocolate brownie, but a peppermint accent adds a refreshing taste.

Brown Sugar Bars ·

1½ cups dark brown sugar,
   packed

1 cup flour

½ cup butter, melted

2 eggs

1 cup chopped pecans

½ teaspoon baking powder

Mix together ½ cup of the sugar, flour, and butter; pat into a greased 8 × 8 × 2-inch pan. Bake in a preheated 350° oven for 15 minutes. Beat eggs well. Add remaining 1 cup sugar, pecans, and baking powder; mix well. Pour over baked batter, return to oven, and bake 20 minutes. Cool; cut into bars. *Do not double recipe.*

YIELD: 2½ DOZEN

Linzer Bars ·

½ cup butter, softened
½ cup brown sugar, packed
¼ cup sugar
⅔ cup almonds, ground and
    toasted
1 egg, beaten
1½ cups flour
¾ teaspoon baking powder
½ teaspoon cinnamon
¼ teaspoon salt
¾ cup seedless raspberry jam
1 teaspoon grated lemon peel
Confectioners' sugar

Cream butter and sugars until mixture is light and fluffy; stir in almonds and egg. Sift together flour, baking powder, cinnamon, and salt. Add dry ingredients to creamed mixture; blend well. Press two-thirds of the dough into a greased 8 × 8 × 2-inch pan; spread with raspberry jam that has been combined with lemon peel. Roll out remaining dough ⅛-inch thick between sheets of waxed paper and chill for 15 minutes. Peel off the top sheet, cut into ½-inch strips, and arrange in a lattice pattern on top of jam. Bake in a preheated 375° oven for 30 minutes. Sift confectioners' sugar evenly over top. Cool; cut into bars.

YIELD: 3 DOZEN

Vienna Raspberry Chocolate Bars ·

1 cup butter, softened
2 egg yolks
1½ cups sugar
2½ cups flour
1 cup seedless raspberry jam
1 cup chocolate chips
4 egg whites
¼ teaspoon salt
2 cups finely chopped nuts

Cream butter with egg yolks and ½ cup sugar. Add flour and knead. Pat batter on a greased 15 × 10-inch jellyroll pan. Bake in a preheated 350° oven for 15 to 20 minutes, until lightly browned. Remove from oven; spread with jam and top with chocolate chips. Whip egg whites with salt until stiff; gradually beat in remaining 1 cup sugar. Fold in nuts. Gently spread egg white mixture on top of jam and chocolate. Bake in a preheated 350° oven for 25 minutes. Cool; cut into bars. Best served the same day.

YIELD: 5 DOZEN

Nutmeg Cake Squares

1½ cups brown sugar, packed

2 cups flour

½ cup cold butter, cut in pieces

1 cup buttermilk

1 teaspoon baking soda

1 egg, beaten

1 teaspoon freshly grated
 nutmeg

¾ cup coarsely chopped
 cashews

Using either pastry blender or food processor, blend sugar and flour; cut butter into dry ingredients to make small crumbs. Press half the crumbs into a greased 9 × 9 × 2-inch pan. Combine buttermilk with baking soda. To remaining crumbs, add egg, nutmeg, and buttermilk mixture. Pour batter over crumb mixture in baking pan and sprinkle with chopped nuts. Bake in a preheated 350° oven for 35 minutes. Cool; cut into squares.

YIELD: 3 DOZEN

White Chocolate and Macadamia Nut Blondies

1 cup butter, softened

2½ cups brown sugar

4 teaspoons instant espresso
 powder

1 tablespoon vanilla

4 eggs

2 cups flour

2 teaspoons salt

2 cups coarsely chopped
 macadamia nuts

2 cups coarsely chopped
 white chocolate

Cream butter, sugar, espresso powder, and vanilla until light and fluffy. Beat in eggs one at a time; continue beating for 2 minutes. Sift together flour and salt; add to creamed mixture and stir until moistened. Fold in nuts and white chocolate. Spread batter in a well greased 13 × 9 × 2-inch pan. Bake in a preheated 350° oven for 40 minutes, or until a tester inserted in the center comes out clean. Let cool in pan; cut into bars.

YIELD: 4 DOZEN

Choco-Peanut Breakaways ·

1 cup butter, softened

1½ cups brown sugar, packed

¼ cup dark corn syrup

2 cups flour

1 cup chocolate chips

1 cup salted peanuts

1 egg

Cream butter and sugar. Stir in remaining ingredients and spread in a greased 15 × 10-inch jellyroll pan. Bake in a preheated 375° oven for 20 to 25 minutes. Do not overbake; a slight imprint should remain when touched with finger. Cut into squares while warm *or* let cool and break away pieces.

YIELD: 5 DOZEN

Nutty Coconut Bars ·

CRUMB MIXTURE

½ cup cold butter, cut in pieces

½ cup brown sugar, packed

1 cup flour

TOPPING

2 eggs

1 cup brown sugar, packed

1 teaspoon vanilla

2 tablespoons flour

½ teaspoon baking powder

¼ teaspoon salt

1½ cups flaked coconut

1 cup chopped pecans

Mix ingredients to a crumbly mass. Pack firmly into a greased 12 × 8 × 2-inch pan. Bake in a preheated 350° oven for 10 to 15 minutes. Meanwhile, prepare topping.

Beat eggs well; add sugar and vanilla. Sift together flour, baking powder, and salt; add to creamed mixture and blend well. Stir in coconut and pecans. Pour over baked crust. Return to 350° oven and bake for 20 minutes. Cool; cut into bars.

YIELD: 3½ DOZEN

Bourbon Pecan Bars

1¼ cups flour

½ teaspoon baking powder

½ teaspoon salt

1 cup chopped toasted pecans

⅓ cup sugar

½ cup cold butter, cut in pieces

3 eggs

1¼ cups brown sugar, packed

¼ cup butter, melted and
   cooled

3 tablespoons bourbon

1 teaspoon vanilla

Salt, to taste

Sift together flour, baking powder, and salt. Add pecans, sugar, and the cold butter. Blend mixture until it resembles meal; press dough into a greased 9 × 9 × 2-inch pan. Bake in a preheated 350° oven for 15 minutes, or until golden brown. Beat eggs, brown sugar, the melted butter, bourbon, vanilla, and salt until the mixture is well combined. Pour over baked layer. Return to 350° oven for 25 minutes, or until puffed and lightly browned. Cool; cut into bars.

YIELD: 3 DOZEN

Date Nut Bars

1 cup flour

1 cup chopped dates

¾ cup sugar

½ cup butter, softened

½ teaspoon cardamom

½ cup chopped nuts

2 eggs

1 teaspoon baking powder

2 teaspoons vanilla

½ teaspoon salt

Combine all ingredients in 1½ quart mixing bowl and stir by hand until mixed (1 to 2 minutes). Spread into a greased 9 × 9 × 2-inch pan. Bake in a preheated 350° oven for 22 to 27 minutes, or until a tester inserted in the center comes out clean. Cool completely; cut into bars.

YIELD: 3 DOZEN

Pecan Turtles

2 cups flour

1½ cups brown sugar, packed

½ cup butter, softened

1 cup whole pecan halves

⅔ cup butter

1 cup milk chocolate chips

Mix flour, 1 cup of the sugar, and the softened butter; blend well. Pat firmly into an *ungreased* 13 × 9 × 2-inch pan. Place pecans evenly over unbaked crust. Combine remaining ⅔ cup butter with the remaining ½ cup sugar in a saucepan; cook over medium heat, stirring constantly until mixture boils. Pour this caramel layer over crust. Bake in a preheated 350° oven for 18 to 22 minutes. Remove from oven and immediately sprinkle with chocolate chips; allow chips to melt slightly and swirl to achieve marbleized effect. Cool completely; cut as desired.

YIELD: 3½ DOZEN

Pecan Bars

1 cup flour

½ teaspoon baking powder

⅓ cup dark brown sugar, packed

¼ cup cold butter, cut in pieces

¼ cup dark brown sugar, packed

3 tablespoons flour

2 eggs, beaten

¾ cup dark corn syrup

½ teaspoon salt

1 teaspoon vanilla

¾ cup pecans, chopped

Sift together 1 cup flour and baking powder. Stir in ⅓ cup sugar. Cut in butter, using pastry blender or food processor until mixture appears dry. Pat evenly into a greased 12 × 8 × 2-inch pan. Bake in a preheated 350° oven for 10 minutes. Blend remaining ¼ cup sugar and remaining flour; set aside. Beat eggs; add corn syrup, flour mixture, salt, and vanilla. Mix well. Pour over partially baked batter and sprinkle with chopped nuts. Return to 350° oven for 25 to 30 minutes. Cut into bars while warm.

YIELD: 3½ DOZEN

Honey Bars ·

½ cup butter, softened

1 cup honey

1 teaspoon vanilla

3 eggs

1¼ cups flour

1 teaspoon baking powder

½ teaspoon salt

1 cup chopped dates

1 cup chopped nuts

Sugar

Cream butter; add honey, vanilla, and eggs. Sift flour with baking powder and salt. Mix with dates and nuts; add to creamed mixture. Spread batter into a greased 13 × 9 × 2-inch pan. Bake in a preheated 350° oven for 30 to 35 minutes. Set on rack to cool; cut into bars and roll in sugar.

YIELD: 4 DOZEN

Zebras ·

1 cup butter, softened

1 cup brown sugar, packed

2 eggs

1 teaspoon vanilla

2 cups flour

1 teaspoon baking powder

1½ cups chocolate chips

¾ cup coarsely chopped
   walnuts

Cream butter and sugar until light and fluffy. Beat in eggs, one at time, beating well after each addition. Beat in vanilla. Stir in sifted flour and baking powder; blend well. Transfer half the batter to another bowl. Melt 1 cup chocolate chips and add to creamed mixture. Spread chocolate mixture into a greased 13 × 9 × 2-inch pan lined with greased and floured foil. Drop spoonfuls of reserved batter over chocolate layer. Spread carefully. Sprinkle with remaining ½ cup chocolate chips and walnuts. Bake in a preheated 350° oven for 30 to 35 minutes. Cool on rack; cut into bars.

YIELD: 4 DOZEN

Bar cookies may be topped with nuts, dusted with confectioners' sugar, or frosted with an appropriate icing. Simply drizzling or piping icing over bars adds a touch of class.

Snow on the Mountain Bars

3 eggs
1 cup sugar
1 teaspoon vanilla
¾ cup flour
1 teaspoon baking powder
½ teaspoon salt
2 cups chopped dates
1 cup chopped walnuts
Confectioners' sugar

Beat eggs until thick and pale yellow. Gradually add sugar, beating well. Blend in vanilla. Sift together flour, baking powder, and salt. Stir dry ingredients into egg mixture, blending well. Fold in dates and walnuts. Pour mixture into a greased 13 × 9 × 2-inch pan. Bake in a preheated 350° oven for 25 minutes. Cool in pan. Sprinkle with confectioners' sugar; cut into bars.

YIELD: 4 DOZEN

Cranberry Crumbles

FILLING
2 cups dried cranberries
1 tablespoon cornstarch
1 cup sugar
¾ cup water
2 tablespoons lemon juice

CRUMB MIXTURE
1½ cups flour
1 teaspoon baking powder
¼ teaspoon salt
1 cup brown sugar, packed
1½ cups quick oatmeal
¾ cup unsalted butter, melted
1 teaspoon vanilla

Combine cranberries, cornstarch, and sugar in saucepan; add water and lemon juice. Cook over low heat, stirring constantly until thick, about 5 minutes. Set aside to cool while preparing crust.

For the crumb mixture, sift flour with baking powder and salt into large mixing bowl. Combine brown sugar and oatmeal with dry ingredients; mix well. Add melted butter and vanilla; blend until light and crumbly. Reserve 1 cup of crumbs. Press remaining mixture on the bottom of a greased 13 × 9 × 2-inch pan. Spread cranberry filling over crust, sprinkle with reserved crumb mixture, and gently pat crumbs over filling. Bake in a preheated 350° oven for 20 to 25 minutes, or until lightly browned. Cut into oblongs while warm.

YIELD: 4 DOZEN

Golden Apricot Bars ·

CRUMB MIXTURE

1½ cups flour

½ cup brown sugar, packed

½ cup cold butter, cut in pieces

FILLING

¾ cup dried apricots, chopped

2 eggs, beaten

1 cup brown sugar, packed

½ teaspoon vanilla

2 tablespoons flour

½ teaspoon baking powder

¼ teaspoon salt

FROSTING

2 tablespoons butter, softened

1½ cups confectioners' sugar

1 to 2 tablespoons light cream

Combine flour and sugar; cut in butter. Pat mixture into a 13 × 9 × 2-inch greased pan. Bake in a preheated 275° oven for 10 minutes.

To make filling, soak apricots in hot water for 6 to 8 minutes; drain well and pat dry. Beat eggs well; add sugar and vanilla. Stir in sifted dry ingredients. Fold apricots into batter. Pour over baked crumb mixture and bake in a preheated 350° oven for 20 minutes. Cool.

For the frosting, cream butter and sugar. Add cream and mix to spreading consistency. Frost bars.

YIELD: 4 DOZEN

Fresh Apple Cake Bars ·

2 cups sugar

2 cups flour

2 tablespoons baking soda

1 teaspoon salt

2 teaspoons cinnamon

2 teaspoons nutmeg

2 eggs, beaten

2 teaspoons vanilla

1 cup vegetable oil

3 cups chopped, *unpeeled* apples

1 cup raisins

Sift together sugar, flour, baking soda, salt, cinnamon, and nutmeg. Beat eggs in a large bowl, add vanilla and oil, and blend well. Combine with dry ingredients. Add apples and raisins. Press into an *ungreased* 17 × 12 × 2-inch pan. Bake in a preheated 350° oven for 35 to 40 minutes. Cool; cut into bars.

YIELD: 7 DOZEN

Sour Cream Apple Squares

2 cups flour

2 cups brown sugar, packed

½ cup butter, softened

1 cup chopped nuts

1½ teaspoon cinnamon

1 teaspoon baking soda

½ teaspoon salt

1 cup sour cream

1 teaspoon vanilla

1 egg

2 cups finely chopped,
   peeled apples

½ cup chopped nuts
   (optional)

In a large bowl, combine flour, sugar, and butter; blend at low speed, just until crumbly. Stir in nuts. Press 2¾ cups crumb mixture into an *ungreased* 13 × 9 × 2-inch pan. To remaining mixture, add cinnamon, baking soda, salt, sour cream, vanilla, and egg; blend well. Stir in apples. Spoon evenly over base. Sprinkle nuts over top, if desired. Bake in a preheated 350° oven for 25 to 30 minutes. Cool; cut into squares.

YIELD: 4 DOZEN

Prune Nut Bars

1 cup chopped prunes

1 cup chopped, peeled apple

⅓ cup dry sherry

6 tablespoons butter, softened

¾ cup brown sugar, packed

1 egg, lightly beaten

1 teaspoon vanilla

1 teaspoon cinnamon

¼ teaspoon allspice

¼ teaspoon cloves

¼ teaspoon nutmeg

½ cup chopped walnuts

¾ cup flour

½ teaspoon baking powder

¼ teaspoon salt

Combine prunes, apples, and sherry; macerate for at least 2 hours. Cream together butter and sugar until the mixture is light and fluffy. Add egg, vanilla, cinnamon, allspice, cloves, and nutmeg; combine and mix well. Stir in the apple-prune mixture and walnuts. Sift together flour, baking powder, and salt; add to batter and stir until just combined. Spoon batter into a greased 9 × 9 × 2-inch pan. Bake in a preheated 350° oven for 30 to 35 minutes, or until lightly brown. Cool; cut into bars.

YIELD: 3 DOZEN

LOUIS LOZOWICK
Still Life #2 (Still Life with Apples), 1929

Pumpkin Bars ·

4 eggs

1 cup vegetable oil

2 cups sugar

1 cup canned pumpkin

2 cups flour

1 teaspoon baking powder

1 teaspoon baking soda

½ teaspoon salt

2 teaspoons cinnamon

½ cup nuts, chopped

½ cup raisins

FROSTING

3 ounces cream cheese,
  softened

6 tablespoons butter, softened

¾ cup confectioners' sugar

1 teaspoon vanilla

1 teaspoon milk

Beat eggs well, add oil and sugar, and continue beating until thoroughly blended. Add pumpkin. Sift together flour, baking powder, baking soda, salt, and cinnamon; stir into pumpkin mixture. Add nuts and raisins. Pour into a greased, floured 17 × 12-inch jellyroll pan. Bake in a preheated 350° oven for 20 to 25 minutes. Cool.

For frosting, cream together cream cheese and butter; gradually add sugar and vanilla. Add enough milk to achieve spreading consistency. Frost cooled cookies and cut into bars.

YIELD: 6 DOZEN

FRANÇOIS BOUCHER, FILS
Plate 8 from *Cahiers d'arabesques*, 1780s

Sour Cream Rhubarb Squares ·

½ cup sugar

½ cup chopped nuts

1 tablespoon butter, melted

1 teaspoon cinnamon

¾ cup brown sugar, packed

½ cup butter, softened

1 egg

1 cup flour

1 teaspoon baking soda

¼ teaspoon salt

1 cup quick oatmeal

1 cup sour cream

1½ cups rhubarb, cut
   in ½-inch pieces

Mix sugar, nuts, the melted butter, and cinnamon; set aside. Cream together brown sugar, remaining ½ cup butter, and egg. Thoroughly stir together flour, baking soda, salt, and oatmeal. Add to creamed mixture alternately with sour cream. Stir in rhubarb. Turn into a greased 13 × 9 × 2-inch pan. Sprinkle with reserved topping. Bake in a preheated 350° oven for 45 minutes.

Make glaze with confectioners' sugar, a dash of cinnamon, and enough milk to thin to the consistency of light cream. Drizzle glaze over cookies while still warm. Cool; cut into squares.

YIELD: 4 DOZEN

Hermits ·

¼ cup vegetable oil

½ cup butter, softened

1 cup sugar

1 egg

¼ cup molasses

2¼ cups flour

2 teaspoons baking soda

¼ teaspoon salt

¾ teaspoon ginger

1 teaspoon cinnamon

¾ teaspoon cloves

1 cup raisins

Sugar

Cream together oil, butter, and sugar. Add egg and then molasses, blending well after each addition. Sift together flour, baking soda, salt, and spices; stir dry ingredients into the creamed mixture. Add raisins. Pour batter into an *ungreased* 17 × 12-inch jellyroll pan and press. Sprinkle sugar over dough. Bake in a preheated 375° oven for 10 minutes. Cool; cut into bars.

YIELD: 6 DOZEN

Chewy old-fashioned raisin and spice hermits originated in colonial New England. As the tale goes, the name arose because they taste better when hidden away like a hermit for a day or two.

Holiday Lebkuchen

2¾ cups flour

½ teaspoon baking soda

1 teaspoon cinnamon

½ teaspoon nutmeg

½ teaspoon cloves

½ cup finely chopped nuts

½ cup finely chopped candied
  mixed fruit

1 egg, slightly beaten

1 cup dark corn syrup

¾ cup brown sugar, packed

1 tablespoon lemon juice

1 teaspoon grated lemon peel

Holiday sprinkles (optional)

LEMON ICING

1½ cups confectioners' sugar

2 tablespoons lemon juice

Sift together flour, baking soda, and spices; stir in nuts and candied fruit. Set aside. Beat egg and add corn syrup, sugar, lemon juice, and peel; mix well. Stir in flour-fruit mixture. Divide dough in half and turn out onto *two* well greased and floured baking sheets. Moisten hand and flatten dough to ⅛-inch thickness (dough will rise during baking). Bake in a preheated 400° oven for 12 to 15 minutes, or until lightly browned and firm to the touch.

To make icing, mix confectioners' sugar and lemon juice to creamy consistency and brush lightly over warm cookies. Decorate with holiday sprinkles, if desired. Cut into bars while still warm. Cover tightly and store until mellow.

YIELD: 5 DOZEN

Praline Grahams

½ cup butter

½ cup margarine

½ cup sugar

1 teaspoon vanilla

12 whole graham crackers

1 cup chopped nuts

Melt together butter, margarine, and sugar; boil 2 minutes. Add vanilla. Meanwhile, break graham crackers along stamped impressions and line a greased 15 × 10-inch jellyroll pan. Sprinkle nuts over crackers. Pour sugar and butter mixture over crackers. Bake in a preheated 350° oven for 10 minutes. Place on rack to cool; separate pieces while warm.

YIELD: 4 DOZEN

English Toffee Squares ·

1 cup brown sugar, packed

2 cups flour

¼ teaspoon salt

1 cup butter

1 egg yolk

1 teaspoon vanilla or
    ½ teaspoon almond extract

1 cup chocolate chips

½ cup chopped nuts

Mix sugar, flour, and salt; cut in butter. Add egg yolk and vanilla *or* almond extract. Spread in a greased 15 × 10-inch jellyroll pan. Bake in a preheated 350° oven for 15 minutes. Melt chocolate chips and spread over cookies; sprinkle with nuts. Cool; cut into squares.

YIELD: 5 DOZEN

Scottish Butter Squares ·

1 cup unsalted butter, softened

⅔ cup sugar

2 teaspoons vanilla

2 cups flour

¼ teaspoon salt

Confectioners' sugar

Cream butter with sugar until smooth. Add vanilla. Gradually blend in flour and salt; mix thoroughly. Pat mixture evenly into an *ungreased* 15 × 10-inch jellyroll pan. Sprinkle top with confectioners' sugar. Bake in a preheated 350° oven for 16 to 18 minutes, until golden. Cool 5 minutes; cut into squares while warm. Store in airtight container.

YIELD: 5 DOZEN

Cheesecake Squares

⅓ cup brown sugar, packed

½ cup chopped walnuts

1 cup flour

⅓ cup butter, melted

8 ounces cream cheese, softened

¼ cup sugar

1 egg

1 tablespoon lemon juice

2 tablespoons cream or milk

1 teaspoon vanilla

Blend brown sugar, walnuts, and flour; mix with butter until crumbly. Save 1 cup of mixture for topping. Place remainder in a lightly greased 8 × 8 × 2-inch pan. Press firmly. Bake at 350° for 12 to 15 minutes. Beat cream cheese and sugar until smooth; add egg, lemon juice, cream, and vanilla. Pour mixture into baked crust. Top with reserved crumbs. Return to 350° oven and bake for 25 minutes. Cool thoroughly; cut into squares. Store in refrigerator.

YIELD: 2½ DOZEN

This is a cheesecake fan's dream—a creamy texture and a rich, savory taste.

Lemon Love Bars

1 cup butter, softened

2¼ cups flour

½ cup confectioners' sugar

4 eggs

2 cups sugar

1 teaspoon baking powder

6 tablespoons fresh lemon juice

Grated peel of 1 lemon

Confectioners' sugar

Blend butter, 2 cups flour, and confectioners' sugar thoroughly. Press dough into a well greased and floured 13 × 9 × 2-inch pan. Bake in the middle of a preheated 350° oven for 10 to 15 minutes. Meanwhile, beat eggs until frothy. Add sugar, remaining ¼ cup flour, baking powder, lemon juice, and lemon peel; beat until smooth. Pour filling into hot crust. Reduce oven to 325° and bake for 20 minutes, or until filling is set. Loosen edge by running a knife around the inside of the pan; place on rack to cool. Cover and refrigerate 4 hours or overnight before cutting. Using a serrated knife, cut into 20 squares; then cut each square diagonally in half. Dust triangles with confectioners' sugar. Serve at room temperature.

YIELD: 3½ DOZEN

Golden Lemon Bars ·

CRUMB MIXTURE

1½ cups flour

½ cup brown sugar, packed

½ cup cold butter, cut in pieces

FILLING

2 eggs

1 cup brown sugar

½ teaspoon vanilla

2 tablespoons flour

½ teaspoon baking powder

1¼ cups flaked coconut

½ cup chopped pecans

LEMON GLAZE

1 cup confectioners' sugar

1½ tablespoons butter,
    softened

2 to 3 teaspoons lemon juice

1 teaspoon grated lemon peel

Combine flour and brown sugar; cut in butter and pat mixture into a greased 13 × 9 × 2-inch pan. Bake in a preheated 375° oven for 10 minutes. Meanwhile, make the filling.

Beat eggs well; add brown sugar and vanilla, blending thoroughly. Add flour, baking powder, coconut, and pecans. Pour over hot crust. Bake at 350° for 20 minutes.

Combine all glaze ingredients and blend until smooth. Spread over hot cookies. Cool; cut into bars.

YIELD: 4 DOZEN

Pedal harp
Made by GODEFROI HOLTZMAN,
active 1781–1794

Drop Cookies

Drop cookies are fast and simple to make, yet these versatile creations are also sophisticated, offering every classic flavor and texture. Drop dough from a spoon onto a baking sheet either prepared as specified in the recipe or simply lined with parchment paper. Your cookies will have a better shape if you use a second spoon to push the dough off the first, or you may use a small ice-cream scoop to make uniform, rounded cookies. Allow adequate space between mounds of dough so the cookies can spread.

Teapot
England, about 1785

Coconut Snowdrops ·

1 cup butter, softened
½ cup sugar
1 egg
¼ cup milk
1 tablespoon vanilla
2 cups flour
1 cup flaked coconut
Confectioners' sugar

Cream butter and sugar; add egg and beat. Stir in milk, vanilla, flour, and coconut; blend to combine. Drop by small spoonfuls 2 inches apart onto an *ungreased* baking sheet. Bake in a preheated 350° oven for 12 to 15 minutes. Cool completely; sprinkle with confectioners' sugar.

YIELD: 3 DOZEN

Angel Kisses ·

4 egg whites
⅛ teaspoon cream of tartar
Salt, to taste
1¼ cups confectioners' sugar
 or 1 cup granulated sugar
½ teaspoon vanilla

Beat egg whites until stiff but not dry; gradually add cream of tartar, salt, sugar, and vanilla. Drop by small spoonfuls onto a baking sheet lined with parchment paper or foil. Bake in a preheated 250° oven for 50 minutes.

YIELD: 4 DOZEN

Sleeping Macaroons ·

4 cups quick oatmeal
2 cups brown sugar, packed
1 cup vegetable oil
2 eggs, beaten
1 teaspoon salt
1 teaspoon almond extract

Combine oatmeal, sugar, and oil in bowl; blend well. Cover and let stand overnight at room temperature. The next morning, add eggs, salt, and almond extract to oatmeal mixture. Blend thoroughly. Drop by small spoonfuls onto a greased baking sheet. Bake in a preheated 325° oven for 15 minutes.

YIELD: 4 DOZEN

Chocolate Meringues

3 egg whites

Salt, to taste

1 cup sugar

1 cup chocolate chips

2 tablespoons cocoa

½ teaspoon vanilla

Beat egg whites with salt until stiff but not dry. Gradually beat in sugar. Fold in chocolate chips, cocoa, and vanilla. Drop batter by small spoonfuls onto a foil-lined baking sheet. Bake in a preheated 275° oven for 30 minutes. Transfer entire foil sheet to rack and allow cookies to cool. Store in airtight container.

YIELD: 4 DOZEN

Date Macaroons

4 egg whites

1½ cups sugar

⅛ teaspoon salt

1 teaspoon vanilla

2 cups pitted dates, chopped

1 cup chopped pecans

Beat egg whites until stiff but not dry. Add sugar and salt gradually; continue beating until mixture holds shape. Blend in vanilla; fold in dates and nuts. Drop by small spoonfuls onto a greased baking sheet. Bake in a preheated 350° oven for 20 minutes.

YIELD: 8 DOZEN

French Nut Drops

2 egg whites

1 cup sugar

1 cup finely chopped walnuts

1 cup finely chopped pecans

Beat egg whites until stiff but not dry. Gradually add sugar until mixture is thoroughly blended and holds shape. Stir in all nuts. Put mixture in top of double boiler over boiling water and stir for 8 minutes, or until hot and slightly thickened. Cool, stirring several times, until cool enough to handle. Drop by small spoonfuls onto a baking sheet lined with parchment paper. Bake in a preheated 350° oven for 15 minutes, or until lightly browned. Allow drops to remain on paper for 1 minute before removing with spatula. Place on rack to cool.

YIELD: 4 DOZEN

Scottish Oat Surprises

1 cup butterscotch chips

1 cup sugar

½ cup butter, softened

1 egg

1 teaspoon vanilla

½ teaspoon almond extract

1 cup flour

½ teaspoon salt

½ teaspoon baking soda

1 cup quick oatmeal

1⅓ cups flaked coconut

Melt butterscotch chips over hot water; set aside. Cream together sugar and butter until light and fluffy. Add egg and beat thoroughly. Blend in melted butterscotch chips, vanilla, and almond extract. Sift together flour, salt, and baking soda; stir into creamed mixture. Stir in oatmeal and coconut. Drop by small spoonfuls onto a lightly greased baking sheet. Bake in a preheated 350° oven for 12 minutes. Remove from baking sheet immediately.

YIELD: 3 DOZEN

Banana Nut Drops

½ cup butter, softened

1 cup sugar

2 eggs

1 cup mashed ripe bananas

1 teaspoon vanilla

2 ¾ cups flour

1½ teaspoons baking soda

½ teaspoon salt

¼ teaspoon cinnamon

½ cup buttermilk

1 cup chopped nuts

Cream together butter and sugar until light and fluffy. Add eggs one at a time, beating well after each addition. Add bananas and vanilla. Sift together flour, baking soda, salt, and cinnamon. Add dry ingredients alternately with buttermilk. Stir in nuts. Drop by small spoonfuls about 2 inches apart onto a greased baking sheet. Bake in a preheated 375° oven for 10 minutes.

YIELD: 6 DOZEN

Soft Ginger Cookies

¾ cup unsalted butter,
   softened
1 cup sugar
¼ cup molasses
1 egg
1¾ cups flour
1 tablespoon baking powder
½ teaspoon salt
1 teaspoon cloves
1 teaspoon ginger
1 teaspoon cinnamon
½ cup finely chopped
   crystallized ginger

Cream butter and sugar; beat in molasses and egg. Sift together flour, baking powder, salt, and spices; stir dry ingredients into creamed mixture. Add crystallized ginger and mix until blended. Drop by small spoonfuls onto an *ungreased* baking sheet. Bake in a preheated 350° oven for 10 to 15 minutes.

YIELD: 2 DOZEN

Sour Cream Cookies

½ cup butter, softened
1½ cups sugar
2 eggs
1 teaspoon vanilla
3½ cups flour
½ teaspoon baking powder
½ teaspoon baking soda
1 cup sour cream
Cinnamon and sugar, sugar
   and chopped nuts, or flaked
   coconut

Cream butter and sugar; add eggs and vanilla and beat thoroughly. Sift together flour, baking powder, and baking soda; beat into first mixture alternately with sour cream. Drop by small spoonfuls onto a greased baking sheet, allowing 1-inch spaces between cookies. Dust with sugar and cinnamon *or* sugar and chopped nuts *or* coconut. Bake in a preheated 350° oven for 12 minutes.

Variation: Divide batter into three parts—leave one part plain, add ⅓ cup chocolate chips to the second part, and add ⅓ cup raisins to the third.

YIELD: 6 DOZEN

Pumpkin Cookies

½ cup butter, softened

1 cup sugar

1 cup canned pumpkin

1 teaspoon vanilla

2 cups flour

1 teaspoon baking powder

1 teaspoon baking soda

1 teaspoon cinnamon

½ teaspoon cloves

½ teaspoon ginger

1 cup raisins

1 cup chopped nuts

Cream butter and sugar. Add pumpkin and vanilla; beat well. Sift together flour, baking powder, baking soda, and spices; stir into pumpkin mixture. Add raisins and nuts; stir to blend. Drop by small spoonfuls onto a greased baking sheet. Bake in a preheated 375° oven for 10 minutes.

YIELD: 5 DOZEN

Orange Cookies

1½ cups sugar

½ cup Crisco (no substitute)

½ cup margarine (no substitute)

2 eggs

4 cups flour

½ teaspoon salt

1 teaspoon baking soda

1½ teaspoon baking powder

1 cup sour cream

ICING

4 cups confectioners' sugar

1 orange, juice and grated peel

1 tablespoon butter, melted

Cream sugar and shortenings. Add eggs and beat well. Sift together flour, salt, baking soda, and baking powder; add alternately with sour cream. Drop by small spoonfuls onto a greased baking sheet. Bake in a preheated 350° oven for 10 to 15 minutes. Cool.

Combine icing ingredients until smooth. Spread over cookies.

YIELD: 6 DOZEN

Lemonade Drops

1 cup butter, softened

1 cup sugar

2 eggs

3 cups flour

1 teaspoon baking soda

¾ cup frozen lemonade
  concentrate, thawed

Sugar

Cream together butter and sugar. Add eggs one at a time, beating well after each addition. Sift together flour and baking soda. Stir dry ingredients into egg mixture alternately with ½ cup of the lemonade concentrate. Drop by small spoonfuls 2 inches apart onto an *ungreased* baking sheet. Bake in upper third of a preheated 400° oven for 8 minutes, or until edges are lightly browned. Remove from oven, brush lightly with remaining concentrate, and sprinkle with sugar. Cool on racks.

YIELD: 4 DOZEN

Cranberry Cookies

½ cup butter, softened

1 cup sugar

¾ cup brown sugar, packed

1 teaspoon vanilla

⅓ cup milk

1 egg

3 cups flour

1 teaspoon baking powder

¼ teaspoon baking soda

½ teaspoon salt

1 cup mixed candied fruit,
  diced

1 teaspoon grated orange peel

2½ cups fresh cranberries,
  chopped

Cream together butter, sugars, and vanilla. Beat in milk and egg. Sift together flour, baking powder, baking soda, and salt; add to creamed mixture and blend well. Stir in the candied fruit, orange peel, and cranberries. For each cookie, use two level tablespoons of batter on a well greased baking sheet, about 2 inches apart. Bake in a preheated 375° oven for 15 to 18 minutes.

YIELD: 3½ DOZEN

Date Cashew Honeys ·

1½ cups *unsifted* flour
½ teaspoon baking powder
½ teaspoon salt
½ cup butter, softened
½ cup brown sugar, packed
¼ cup honey
1 egg
1 teaspoon vanilla
1 cup chopped pitted dates
1⅓ cups chopped cashews

Sift together flour, baking powder, and salt; set aside. Cream together butter and sugar in a bowl until light and fluffy. Add honey, egg, and vanilla, beating until well blended. Add dry ingredients to creamed mixture, combining well. Stir in dates and cashews. Drop by small spoonfuls onto a greased baking sheet. Bake in a preheated 400° oven for 10 to 12 minutes, or until lightly browned.

YIELD: 3½ DOZEN

Chocolate Walnut Wafers ·

½ cup butter, softened
1 cup sugar
2 eggs, well beaten
2 ounces unsweetened
    chocolate, melted
¼ teaspoon vanilla
⅔ cup flour
¼ teaspoon salt
1 cup chopped walnuts

Cream butter; add sugar gradually. Add eggs, beating well. Add chocolate, vanilla, flour, and salt. Add nuts. Drop by small spoonfuls 1 inch apart onto a greased baking sheet. Bake in a preheated 350° oven for 8 to 10 minutes.

YIELD: 3 DOZEN

OPPOSITE: JOHN SINGLETON COPLEY
Paul Revere, 1768

Brownie Drops ·

2 bars (4 ounces each)
    German chocolate

1 tablespoon butter

2 eggs

¾ cup sugar

½ teaspoon vanilla

¼ cup flour

¼ teaspoon baking powder

¼ teaspoon cinnamon

½ teaspoon salt

¾ cup finely chopped nuts

Melt chocolate and butter in a double boiler over hot water; set aside to cool. Beat eggs until foamy. Add sugar, 2 tablespoons at a time; beat until thick and pale yellow. Blend in chocolate and vanilla. Sift together flour, baking powder, cinnamon, and salt; add to chocolate mixture and blend well. Add chopped nuts. Drop by small spoonfuls onto a greased baking sheet. Bake in a preheated 350° oven for 8 to 10 minutes.

YIELD: 2 DOZEN

Chocolate Fruit Drops ·

½ cup butter, softened

1 cup sugar

1 egg

2 ounces unsweetened
    chocolate, melted and
    cooled

¾ cup buttermilk

1 teaspoon vanilla

1¾ cups flour

½ teaspoon salt

½ teaspoon baking soda

1 cup chopped pecans

1 cup cut-up dates

1 cup candied cherries

Cream butter and sugar; add egg and blend well. Add chocolate. Stir in buttermilk and vanilla. Sift together and stir in flour, salt, and baking soda. Stir in nuts, dates, and cherries. Chill dough. Drop dough by small spoonfuls about 2 inches apart onto an *ungreased* baking sheet. Bake in a preheated 350° oven for 10 to 12 minutes. Cool.

YIELD: 5 DOZEN

For a spectacular presentation, spread white or chocolate icing over tops. Garnish with additional cherries or nuts.

Brownie Chocolate Chip Cookies · · · · · · · · · · · ·

½ cup butter, softened

1 cup sugar

2 eggs

2 ounces unsweetened
chocolate, melted

½ teaspoon vanilla

1 cup flour

2 cups chocolate chips

½ cup chopped walnuts

Cream butter and sugar; add eggs, melted chocolate, vanilla, and flour. Add chocolate chips and nuts. Drop by small spoonfuls onto a greased baking sheet. Bake in a preheated 350° oven for 10 minutes.

YIELD: 3 DOZEN

Chocolate Peanut Drops · · · · · · · · · · · · · · ·

1 cup brown sugar, packed

½ cup butter, softened

1 teaspoon vanilla

1 egg

1½ cups flour

¾ teaspoon baking soda

½ teaspoon baking powder

½ teaspoon salt

¼ cup milk

1 cup chocolate chips

1 cup chopped salted peanuts

Cream sugar, butter, and vanilla; add egg and mix thoroughly. Sift together flour, baking soda, baking powder, and salt; add to creamed mixture alternately with milk. Stir in chocolate chips and peanuts. Drop by small spoonfuls onto a greased baking sheet. Bake in a preheated 375° oven for 10 to 12 minutes.

YIELD: 3½ DOZEN

Needless Markup Cookies ·

1 cup butter, softened

1 cup sugar

1 cup brown sugar, packed

2 eggs

1 teaspoon vanilla

2½ cups old fashioned oatmeal

2 cups flour

½ teaspoon salt

1 teaspoon baking powder

1 teaspoon baking soda

2 cups chocolate chips

4 ounces milk chocolate, finely grated

1½ cup chopped pecans

Cream together butter and sugars. Add eggs and vanilla; blend well. Pulverize oatmeal in a food processor and add to mixture. Sift together flour, salt, baking powder, and baking soda; add and mix well. Add chocolate chips, grated milk chocolate, and nuts. Drop by small spoonfuls onto a greased baking sheet. Bake in a preheated 350° oven for 10 to 12 minutes; do not overbake. Cool 2 minutes before removing from sheet.

YIELD: 5 DOZEN

Bearing the good-humored nickname for Neiman Marcus, this recipe is one among several said to be for the department store's famous cookies.

White Chocolate and Cashew Cookies ·

½ cup butter, softened

1 cup brown sugar, packed

1 egg

1¾ cups flour

¼ teaspoon salt

¾ teaspoon baking soda

½ cup sour cream

2 cups white chocolate chunks

1 cup cashew nuts

Cream butter and sugar; add egg and beat well. Sift together flour, salt, and baking soda; add dry ingredients alternately with sour cream. Stir in chocolate and cashews. Drop by small spoonfuls 2 inches apart onto a baking sheet lined with parchment paper. Bake in a preheated 375° oven for 12 to 14 minutes. Cool on racks.

YIELD: 5 DOZEN

Chocolate Chocolate Chip Cookies

⅔ cup flour

⅓ cup cocoa

1 teaspoon baking powder

½ teaspoon salt

½ cup unsalted butter, softened

½ cup brown sugar, packed

½ cup sugar

1 egg

1 teaspoon vanilla

1 cup chocolate chips

½ cup chopped pecans or walnuts

Sift together flour, cocoa, baking powder, and salt; set aside. Cream butter, add sugars, and blend thoroughly. Add egg and vanilla; mix well. Stir in dry ingredients, chocolate chips, and nuts. Drop by small spoonfuls onto a lightly greased baking sheet. Bake in a 350° oven for 10 to 12 minutes. Do not overbake; a slight imprint should remain when touched with finger.

YIELD: 3 DOZEN

Brown Sugar Nut Cookies

1 cup butter, softened

1 cup brown sugar, packed

½ teaspoon vanilla

1 egg

1½ cups flour

½ cup chopped pecans

Cream butter and sugar until light and fluffy. Add vanilla and egg; beat well. Mix in flour and pecans. Drop by small spoonfuls 2 inches apart onto a greased baking sheet. Bake in a preheated 350° oven for 10 to 12 minutes.

YIELD: 3½ DOZEN

Toffee Crunch Cookies ·

2½ cups flour

1 teaspoon baking powder

1 teaspoon baking soda

1 teaspoon salt

1 cup butter, softened

1 cup sugar

1 cup dark brown sugar,
   packed

1 tablespoon vanilla

2 eggs, slightly beaten

1¾ cups English toffee bits

2 cups white chocolate chips

3 cups coarsely chopped
   walnuts

Sift together flour, baking powder, baking soda, and salt; set aside. In a large mixing bowl, cream butter and sugars until well blended. Add vanilla and eggs; beat well. Gradually mix in dry ingredients. Stir in toffee bits, white chocolate chips, and walnuts. Drop batter by small spoonfuls onto a baking sheet either well greased or lined with parchment paper. Bake in a preheated 350° oven for 10 to 12 minutes, or until golden brown. Cool slightly and remove from baking sheet.

YIELD: 5 DOZEN

Sesame Seed Cookies ·

1 teaspoon butter

½ cup sesame seeds

¾ cup vegetable oil

1½ cups dark brown sugar,
   packed

2 eggs

½ teaspoon vanilla

1½ cups *unsifted* whole wheat
   flour

½ teaspoon baking powder

½ teaspoon salt

Melt butter in a heavy frying pan over low heat. Add sesame seeds and stir until golden brown; set aside. Cream oil and brown sugar until smooth; beat in eggs and vanilla. Stir together flour, baking powder, and salt. Add to creamed mixture; mix until well blended. Stir in toasted sesame seeds. Drop by small spoonfuls onto a lightly greased baking sheet. Bake in a preheated 325° oven for 8 minutes.

YIELD: 5 DOZEN

Simple decorations can indicate a cookie's flavor. Give your drop cookies a professional flair. Before baking, sprinkle tops with spiced sugar, crystal sugar, or flavored nonpareils and press gently into dough. You may instead want to enhance the appearance of baked cookies with a small amount of frosting, using a spatula to spread the frosting in a pretty swirl.

Walnut Chews

3 cups Total cereal
2 cups flour
½ teaspoon baking soda
½ teaspoon salt
¾ cup butter, softened
2 cups brown sugar, packed
2 eggs
1 cup coarsely chopped
    walnuts

Measure cereal, crush to 1½ cups, and set aside. Sift together flour, baking soda, and salt; set aside. Cream butter and sugar until light and fluffy. Add eggs and beat well. Add sifted dry ingredients, nuts, and crushed cereal; mix thoroughly. Drop by small spoonfuls about 2 inches apart onto a lightly greased baking sheet. Bake in a preheated 350° oven for 15 minutes, or until lightly browned. Remove immediately from baking sheet; cool on wire racks.

YIELD: 4½ DOZEN

Pine Nut Cookies

½ cup unsalted butter,
    softened
½ cup sugar
1 egg yolk
1 teaspoon vanilla
1 cup flour
½ cup toasted pine nuts

Cream butter and sugar; beat in egg yolk and vanilla. Add flour and mix in nuts. Drop small spoonfuls of batter onto a greased and floured baking sheet. Bake in a preheated 300° oven for 20 to 25 minutes. While still hot, remove to rack and cool.

YIELD: 2½ DOZEN

Peanut Butter Crinkles ·

¼ cup butter, softened

½ cup smooth peanut butter

½ cup brown sugar, packed

½ cup sugar

1 egg

1 cup flour

½ teaspoon salt

1 teaspoon baking soda

Cream butter and peanut butter until soft. Add sugars gradually, continuing to cream until light and fluffy. Add egg; beat well. Sift flour, salt, and baking soda together; add in two parts, beating well after each addition. Drop by small spoonfuls 2 inches apart onto an *ungreased* baking sheet. Press each cookie with a fork; press again so that ridges are at right angles. Bake in a preheated 350° oven for 8 to 10 minutes.

YIELD: 4½ DOZEN

Michigan Rocks ·

3 cups dates

½ cup flour

¾ cup butter, softened

1½ cups sugar

1 tablespoon cinnamon

½ teaspoon cloves

1 tablespoon water

2¼ cups sifted cake flour

½ teaspoon salt

½ teaspoon baking soda

4 eggs

6 cups walnuts, coarsely
   chopped

4 cups pecans, coarsely
   chopped

Cut dates in half and mix with ½ cup flour. Cream butter and sugar; add spices and water, combining until blended. Sift together cake flour, salt, and baking soda. Add eggs one at a time alternately with dry ingredients. Mix well after each addition. Add nuts and floured dates. Drop by small spoonfuls onto a lightly greased baking sheet. Bake in a preheated 400° oven for 8 minutes.

YIELD: 6 TO 7 DOZEN

Melted Moments ·

1 cup butter, softened

¼ cup confectioners' sugar

1 teaspoon vanilla

½ teaspoon salt

2 cups flour

FROSTING

2 tablespoons butter, softened

1½ cups confectioners' sugar

1 to 2 tablespoons brewed
  coffee, cooled

Cream butter until very light. Add sugar gradually. Add vanilla and salt. Add flour, a little at a time, beating thoroughly until fluffy. Drop by small spoonfuls onto a greased baking sheet. Bake in a preheated 275° oven for 25 to 30 minutes. Cool.

For the frosting, cream butter and sugar. Add coffee and mix to spreading consistency. Frost cookies.

YIELD: 4 DOZEN

Updated for your enjoyment, this outstanding 1849 recipe came from the kitchen of an Australian country woman.

Mocha Divines ·

2 ounces unsweetened
  chocolate

2 tablespoons butter

¼ cup flour

¼ teaspoon baking powder

¼ teaspoon salt

2 eggs

¾ cup sugar

2 tablespoons instant coffee
  powder

1 cup chocolate chips

1 cup chopped nuts

Melt chocolate and butter. Sift together flour, baking powder, and salt; set aside. Beat together eggs, sugar, and coffee powder. Add cooled chocolate and butter to egg mixture. Stir in dry ingredients. Add chocolate chips and nuts. Drop by small spoonfuls 1 inch apart onto a greased baking sheet. Bake in a preheated 350° oven for 10 minutes.

YIELD: 2½ DOZEN

Crisp Spice Cookies · · · · · · · · · · · ·

1½ cups butter, softened

2 cups sugar

2 eggs

½ cup molasses

3 cups flour

1 tablespoon baking soda

2 teaspoons cinnamon

2 teaspoons cloves

2 tablespoons ginger

Cream butter and sugar; add eggs and molasses and blend thoroughly. Sift flour with baking soda, cinnamon, cloves, and ginger, and stir into creamed mixture. Drop by small spoonfuls about 3 inches apart onto a greased baking sheet. Bake in a preheated 375° oven for 10 to 12 minutes.

YIELD: 6 DOZEN

Bourbon Drops · · · · · · · · · · · ·

¼ cup butter, softened

¾ cup sugar

2 eggs

½ cup molasses

2 cups flour

1½ teaspoons baking soda

½ teaspoon cloves

½ teaspoon cinnamon

1½ tablespoons milk

6 tablespoons bourbon

1 cup chopped nuts

2 cups raisins

Cream butter and sugar; add eggs one at a time and beat well after each addition. Sift together flour, baking soda, and spices. To the creamed mixture add molasses, dry ingredients, milk, and bourbon. Stir in nuts and raisins. Drop by small spoonfuls onto a greased baking sheet. Bake in a preheated 350° oven for 12 minutes.

YIELD: 6 DOZEN

JUAN GRIS
Still Life with a Mandolin, 1925

Chocolate Lace Cookies ·

1 egg, beaten

¼ cup brown sugar, packed

¼ cup sugar

1 cup old fashioned oatmeal

½ teaspoon salt

¼ teaspoon almond extract

1 tablespoon unsalted butter,
   melted and cooled

⅔ cup chocolate chips

Beat egg and sugars until mixture is thick and pale. Add oatmeal, salt, almond extract, and butter; stir until well combined. Drop by small spoonfuls 3 inches apart onto a baking sheet lined with greased foil; flatten each mound with back of fork dipped in water. Bake in the middle of a preheated 325° oven for 7 minutes, or until golden brown. Let cookies cool on foil and gently peel away. Melt chocolate in top of double boiler. Dip each cookie into chocolate to coat half. Cool on racks.

YIELD: 2 DOZEN

Irish Lace Cookies ·

¾ cup brown sugar, packed

½ cup butter, softened

2 tablespoons flour

2 tablespoons milk

1 teaspoon vanilla

1½ cups old fashioned oatmeal

Cream sugar and butter well. Beat in flour, milk, and vanilla. Stir in oatmeal and mix well. Drop the mixture by small spoonfuls 2 inches apart onto an *ungreased* baking sheet. Bake in a preheated 350° oven for 10 minutes. Remove from oven and let stand for 1 minute until firm enough to handle with spatula. Turn cookies over and quickly roll them into cylinders. (If they get too stiff to roll, return them to the oven to soften.)

YIELD: 3 DOZEN

Old fashioned oatmeal gives baked goods a distinctive texture and a hearty flavor. Cookies made with quick oatmeal will not spread as thinly as those made with old fashioned oatmeal.

Lacy Hazelnut Cookies ·

1¼ cups chopped, skinned
   hazelnuts

⅔ cup sugar

3 tablespoons flour

1 tablespoon cornstarch

Salt, to taste

3 tablespoons butter, melted
   and cooled

1 teaspoon vanilla

1 teaspoon cinnamon

3 egg whites

Mix hazelnuts, sugar, flour, cornstarch, and salt in a large bowl. Blend butter, vanilla, and cinnamon in a small bowl. Add butter mixture to hazelnut mixture and blend well. Add egg whites and mix until smooth. Chill 30 minutes. Drop batter onto a greased baking sheet by half teaspoons, 2 inches apart. Dip small metal spatula into cold water. Spread cookies to width of 1¼ inches, moistening spatula for each cookie. Bake in a preheated 400° oven until cookies are deep golden and spread 2 inches wide, about 7 to 8 minutes. Transfer to rack using spatula. Cool before serving. Store in airtight container.

YIELD: 6 DOZEN

The terms "hazelnuts" and "filberts" are used interchangeably. Hazelnut describes the wild nut, while filbert refers to the cultivated variety. These nuts have a bitter brown skin. For directions to remove skins, see Hazelnut Biscotti with Black Pepper (page 172).

Guitar
Made by ALEXANDRE VOBOAM,
active 1652–1680

Shaped cookies add an artistic feature to the tea tray. Work dough with hands or fingers to form balls and logs, or roll dough to create imprints and cutouts. This showcase collection of molded, refrigerator, and rolled cookies provides an outstanding repertoire of stylish sweets and pleasant surprises for everyone's taste.

Shaped Cookies

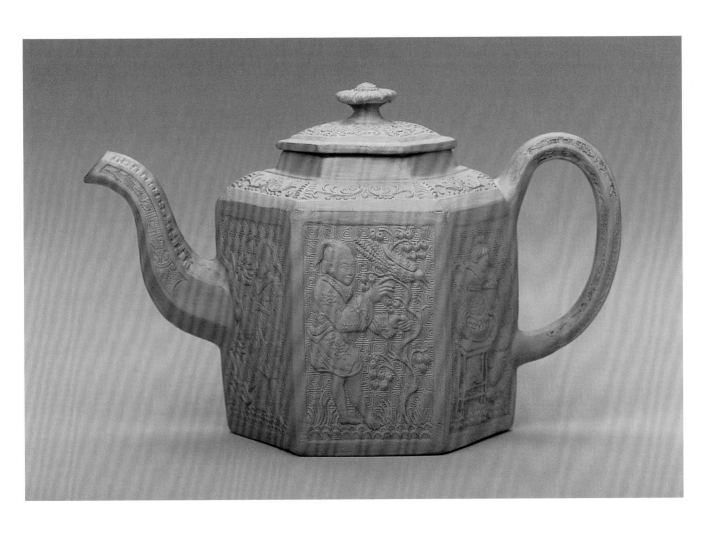

Teapot
England (Staffordshire), about 1750

Molded Cookies

The moderately stiff dough for molded cookies is generally worked at room temperature, although sometimes it must be chilled until firm enough to handle. Bake the cookies until they are lightly browned or until a slight imprint remains from a gentle touch of your finger.

Apricot Balls

2 cups dried apricots
1¼ cups sweetened condensed milk
5⅓ cups flaked coconut
1 teaspoon vanilla

Finely chop apricots. Add milk, coconut, and vanilla; blend well. Form into 1-inch balls and place on a greased baking sheet. Bake in a preheated 325° oven for 8 to 10 minutes.

YIELD: 2 TO 3 DOZEN

Apricot Buttons

FILLING
⅓ cup dried apricots
Water to cover
⅓ cup sugar

DOUGH
½ cup butter, softened
⅓ cup sugar
1 egg yolk
½ teaspoon vanilla
1 cup flour
½ teaspoon salt
1 egg white
Chopped nuts

To make filling, cook apricots until water is absorbed. Add sugar, mix well, and cook for 5 to 10 minutes over medium heat, stirring occasionally until mixture reaches consistency of jam. Let cool and set aside.

For the dough, cream butter and sugar thoroughly. Stir in egg yolk and vanilla. Sift together flour and salt and combine with creamed mixture. Shape into small balls. Dip balls into unbeaten egg white and roll them in chopped nuts. Place 2 inches apart on a lightly greased baking sheet. Depress center. Bake in a preheated 300° oven for 30 minutes. Fill warm centers with cooled apricot filling.

YIELD: 3 DOZEN

Thimble Cookies ·

1½ cups butter, softened
1 cup sugar
3 egg yolks
3 cups flour
Marmalade or jam
Finely chopped nuts
   (optional)

Cream butter, add sugar gradually, and beat until smooth. Add egg yolks and mix well; stir in flour. Chill until firm enough to handle. Form into 1-inch balls, place on a lightly greased baking sheet, and depress the center of each with a thimble. Fill depression with marmalade; garnish with chopped nuts, if desired. Bake in a preheated 350° oven for 15 minutes.

YIELD: 5 DOZEN

Whiskey Crescents ·

1 cup butter, softened
½ cup sugar
2½ cups flour
2 tablespoons rye whiskey
½ cup ground pecans
Confectioners' sugar

Cream butter, add sugar, and mix until light and fluffy. Add flour, whiskey, and nuts. Shape into crescents and place on a lightly greased baking sheet. Bake in a preheated 425° oven for 12 minutes, or until golden. Sprinkle with confectioners' sugar while warm.

YIELD: 5 DOZEN

Christmas Cookies ·

1 cup butter, softened
1½ cups sugar
2 eggs, beaten
2½ cups flour
1 teaspoon baking soda
2 teaspoons cream of tartar
½ teaspoon salt
Colored sugar or cinnamon
   sugar
Nut halves

Cream butter and sugar; add eggs and blend well. Sift together flour, baking soda, cream of tartar, and salt. Stir dry ingredients into butter mixture and chill overnight. Form into 1½-inch balls; roll in colored sugar *or* cinnamon sugar. Place on a greased baking sheet and a press a nut half into center of each. Bake in a preheated 350° oven for 10 minutes.

YIELD: 5 DOZEN

Sensational Swedish Slims

¾ cup butter, softened
¾ cup sugar
1 tablespoon molasses
1½ cups flour
1½ teaspoons baking soda

TOPPING
1 egg, lightly beaten
Sugar
¾ cup sliced almonds
Currants (optional)

Combine all ingredients and work mixture together until well blended. Divide dough into four sections. Roll each section into a rope nearly the length of a baking sheet. Put two ropes on each of *two* lightly greased baking sheets. Press dough with heel of hand until each rope is about 4 to 5 inches wide and 12 inches long. Keep ropes well separated; do not place them close to edge of pan.

Brush each rope with beaten egg and sprinkle with sugar; press sliced almonds into dough and, if desired, add currants. Bake in a preheated 375° oven about 10 minutes, or until light brown. Remove from oven and cut into 1-inch strips. Cool on rack. Store in tightly covered tin.

YIELD: 4 DOZEN

Serve on a pretty tray stacked like Lincoln Logs.

Oatmeal Sugar Cookies

½ cup butter, softened
½ cup brown sugar, packed
½ cup sugar
1 egg
½ teaspoon vanilla
½ teaspoon almond extract
½ teaspoon baking soda,
    dissolved in 2 teaspoons
    apple cider vinegar
1¼ cups flour
¾ cup quick oatmeal
Sugar

Cream butter and sugars until light and fluffy. Blend in egg, vanilla, almond extract, and the baking soda in vinegar. Add flour and oatmeal. Chill dough 1 hour. Roll dough to form 1-inch balls; place on an *ungreased* baking sheet. Flatten with the bottom of a glass dipped in sugar. Bake in a preheated 350° oven for about 12 minutes.

YIELD: 4 DOZEN

Oatmeal Crisps

1 cup butter

2 tablespoons water

2 tablespoons maple syrup

1 cup flour

1½ cups sugar

1 teaspoon baking powder

½ teaspoon baking soda

2½ cups quick oatmeal

Melt butter with water. Add syrup. Sift together flour, 1 cup sugar, baking powder, and baking soda; add oatmeal and mix thoroughly. Combine butter mixture with dry ingredients and chill. Form dough into 1-inch balls and roll in remaining ½ cup sugar. Place on an *ungreased* baking sheet and flatten slightly. Bake in a preheated 350° oven for 12 to 15 minutes. Remove from sheet immediately.

YIELD: 6 DOZEN

Buttery Brandy Wreaths

⅔ cup butter, softened

⅓ cup sugar

1 egg

2 tablespoons grated
    lemon peel

2 tablespoons brandy

2¼ cups flour

1 teaspoon nutmeg

½ teaspoon salt

GLAZE

1¼ cups confectioners' sugar

⅛ teaspoon salt

⅛ teaspoon nutmeg

1 tablespoon milk

1 tablespoon brandy

Red and green candied
    cherries (optional)

Cream butter and sugar; add egg, lemon peel, and brandy. Sift together flour, nutmeg, and salt; combine with creamed mixture. Shape dough into 1-inch balls and then form balls into 4-inch rolls. Shape rolls into circles to make wreaths; place on a lightly greased baking sheet. Bake in a preheated 350° oven for 8 to 12 minutes, until edges are lightly browned. Cool.

Combine all glaze ingredients and stir until smooth. Frost cookies with glaze. If desired, decorate with chopped red and green candied cherries to form a sprig of holly.

YIELD: 5 DOZEN

Brown Sugar Cookies ·

1 cup butter, softened
2 cups brown sugar, packed
2 eggs
1 teaspoon vanilla
3 cups flour
1 teaspoon baking powder
⅛ teaspoon salt

Cream butter and sugar; add eggs one at a time. Mix in vanilla. Sift flour with baking powder and salt; add to creamed mixture and blend well. Form into 1-inch balls and place 2 inches apart on a greased baking sheet; press flat with a fork dipped in flour. Bake in a preheated 350° oven for 8 minutes. Watch carefully; the cookies should be lightly browned.

YIELD: 6 DOZEN

No Roll Sugar Cookies ·

1 cup unsalted butter, softened
1 cup confectioners' sugar
1 egg, beaten
1 teaspoon vanilla
½ teaspoon salt
2 cups flour
Sugar

Cream butter and sugar until light and fluffy. Add egg, vanilla, and salt. Add flour in three additions, blending well. Chill. Form into 1-inch balls and place 2 inches apart on an *ungreased* baking sheet. Dip a glass bottom first in water, then in sugar, and use to flatten each cookie. Bake in a preheated 375° oven for 15 minutes.

YIELD: 4 DOZEN

Benne Wafers ·

¼ cup sesame seeds
1 tablespoon butter, softened
½ cup brown sugar, packed
1 egg yolk
1 teaspoon vanilla
½ teaspoon salt
3 tablespoons flour

Lightly brown sesame seeds in a heavy pan over moderate heat. Combine butter and sugar; add sesame seeds, egg yolk, vanilla, and salt. Add flour and mix well. Wet hands and shape dough into ½-inch balls. Place 2 inches apart on a lightly greased foil-lined baking sheet. Bake on the middle rack in a preheated 350° oven for 7 to 10 minutes, or until firm. Cool completely before peeling foil from wafers.

YIELD: 3 DOZEN

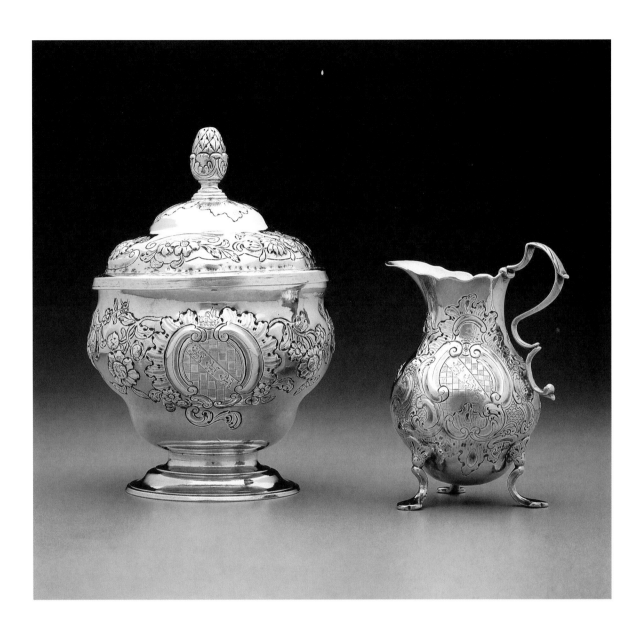

Sugar bowl and creampot
Made by PAUL REVERE, 1735–1818

Crunchy Pecan Cookies ·

1 cup butter, softened
1 cup brown sugar, packed
2 eggs
1 teaspoon vanilla
2 cups *unsifted* flour
1 teaspoon baking powder
¼ teaspoon salt
1 cup butterscotch chips
1 cup chopped pecans
Pecan halves

Cream butter and sugar. Add eggs and vanilla; mix well. Sift together flour, baking powder, and salt; add to creamed mixture. Stir in butterscotch chips and chopped pecans. Shape dough into 1½-inch balls and place on an *ungreased* baking sheet; press a pecan half into the center of each ball. Bake in a preheated 350° oven for 12 to 15 minutes.

YIELD: 7 DOZEN

Pecan Cookies ·

2 cups ground pecans
⅔ cup sugar
½ teaspoon salt
2 unbeaten egg whites
⅓ cup seedless raspberry
    preserves
Candied cherries, halved

Combine pecans, sugar, and salt. Add egg whites and mix until evenly moistened. Form into small balls. Place on an *ungreased* baking sheet. Depress the center of each ball. Fill with preserves and top with cherry half. Bake in a preheated 350° oven for 15 minutes. Remove from sheet at once.

YIELD: 3 DOZEN

Pecan Balls ·

1 cup butter, softened
½ cup sugar
1 teaspoon vanilla
2 cups sifted cake flour
1 cup finely ground pecans
Confectioners' sugar

Cream butter and sugar until light and fluffy; add vanilla. Blend in flour. Mix in pecans. Roll into small balls and place on a lightly greased baking sheet. Bake in a preheated 325° oven for 15 minutes, or until faintly brown. Roll while warm in confectioners' sugar.

YIELD: 4 DOZEN

German Pretzel Cookies ·

⅔ cup butter, softened

1 cup sugar

3 eggs

½ teaspoon vanilla

3 cups flour

¼ teaspoon salt

½ cup finely chopped nuts

Cream butter and ½ cup sugar until light and fluffy. Add 2 eggs, one at a time, beating well after each addition. Beat in vanilla. Sift together flour and salt; add to creamed ingredients, mixing well. Knead dough until smooth. Cover and let rest 1 hour at room temperature. Combine remaining ½ cup sugar with nuts; set aside. Roll a tablespoon of dough on a floured surface to form a slender rope. Form into a pretzel shape or other design, such as a heart or initial. Beat remaining egg slightly. Brush top of each cookie with beaten egg and sprinkle with nut mixture. Place on an *ungreased* baking sheet. Bake in a preheated 325° oven for 25 minutes.

YIELD: 3 DOZEN

White Chocolate and Macadamia Nut Cookies ·

⅔ cup flaked coconut

2¼ cups *unsifted* flour

¼ teaspoon baking powder

1 teaspoon baking soda

1 teaspoon salt

1½ cups unsalted butter, softened

¾ cup brown sugar, packed

¾ cup sugar

1 egg

2 teaspoons vanilla

2 cups white chocolate chunks

1 cup salted macadamia nuts, chopped

Mix coconut and ¼ cup flour in a food processor; set aside. Sift together remaining 2 cups flour, baking powder, baking soda, and salt. Cream butter and sugars until light and fluffy. Beat in egg and vanilla. Gradually add coconut and flour mixtures to the creamed mixture. Stir in chocolate and nuts. Chill overnight. Roll into 1-inch balls; place 2 inches apart on a greased baking sheet. Bake in a preheated 350° oven for 10 to 12 minutes. Cool on rack.

YIELD: 8 DOZEN

Chocolate Crinkles

½ cup butter, softened

1⅔ cups sugar

2 teaspoons vanilla

2 eggs

2 ounces unsweetened
   chocolate, melted

2 cups flour

2 teaspoons baking powder

½ teaspoon salt

⅓ cup milk

½ cup chopped nuts

Confectioners' sugar

Thoroughly cream together butter, sugar, and vanilla. Beat in eggs, then chocolate. Sift together flour, baking powder, and salt; add to creamed mixture alternately with milk, blending well after each addition. Stir in nuts. Chill 2 to 3 hours. Form dough into 1-inch balls; roll in confectioners' sugar. Place 2 to 3 inches apart on a greased baking sheet. Bake in a preheated 350° oven for 15 minutes.

YIELD: 4 DOZEN

Chocolate Chip Snowballs

¾ cup butter, softened

¼ cup sugar

Grated peel of 1 orange

1 teaspoon water

⅛ teaspoon salt

1¾ cups flour

1 cup mini chocolate chips

1 cup finely chopped pecans

Juice of 1 orange

Sugar

Cream butter and ¼ cup sugar until light and fluffy. Add orange peel, water, salt, and flour; mix well. Blend in chocolate chips and pecans. Roll dough into 1-inch balls and place on a lightly greased baking sheet. Bake in a preheated 350° oven for 15 to 20 minutes, or until golden. Cool cookies completely, dip in orange juice, and coat thoroughly with additional sugar. Place on rack to dry so that a sugar crust forms over cookies.

YIELD: 6 DOZEN

Mocha Rum Balls ·

2 cups flour

2 teaspoons instant coffee
   powder

⅛ teaspoon salt

½ cup cocoa

⅔ cup sugar

2 cups chopped nuts

2 tablespoons dark rum

1 teaspoon cold water

1¼ cups butter, softened

Confectioners' sugar

Thoroughly mix all ingredients, except confectioners' sugar. This can be done in a food processor. Chill for 1 hour or overnight. Shape dough into 1-inch balls. Place about 1 inch apart on a lightly greased baking sheet. Bake in a preheated 325° oven for 15 to 18 minutes. Roll in confectioners' sugar while warm, then again when cooled.

YIELD: 5 TO 6 DOZEN

Nutmeg Cookie Logs ·

3 cups flour

1 teaspoon nutmeg

1 cup butter, softened

2 teaspoons vanilla

2 teaspoons dark rum

¾ cup sugar

1 egg

FROSTING

3 tablespoons butter, softened

½ teaspoon vanilla

1 teaspoon dark rum

2½ cups confectioners' sugar

2 to 3 tablespoons cream

Sift together flour and nutmeg; set aside. Cream butter with vanilla and rum. Gradually add sugar, creaming well; blend in egg. Add dry ingredients and mix thoroughly. On a lightly floured surface, shape pieces of dough into long rolls ½ inch in diameter. Cut into 3-inch lengths. Place on an *ungreased* baking sheet. Bake in a preheated 350° oven for 12 minutes. Cool.

    To make frosting, cream butter, vanilla, and rum. Add sugar alternately with cream, beating until spreading consistency. Frost cookies and mark frosting with tines of fork to resemble bark. Sprinkle with nutmeg.

YIELD: 4 DOZEN

When following the next two recipes, hold the cookie press upright, force out the dough until it appears at the edge of the mold, release the pressure quickly, and lift the press away. Use a cold, ungreased baking sheet; otherwise, the shortening in the dough will melt and the cookies will pull away from the sheet as the press is being lifted.

Sherry Tumblers

1 cup butter, softened

2 cups sugar

3 eggs

1 teaspoon vanilla

3 tablespoons sherry

3 cups flour

Cream butter; add sugar gradually while continuing to cream. Beat until light and fluffy. Add eggs and mix well; add vanilla and sherry. Combine flour a little at a time, mixing well after each addition. Chill dough until firm; fill cookie press and force dough through press onto a cold, *ungreased* baking sheet. Bake in a preheated 400° oven for 15 minutes.

YIELD: 8 DOZEN

Velvet Spritz Cookies

1 cup butter, softened

⅔ cup sugar

2 egg yolks, beaten

2½ cups sifted cake flour

1 teaspoon almond extract

Cream butter, add sugar, beat thoroughly. Add beaten egg yolks, flour, and extract. Fill cookie press; force dough through press onto a cold, *ungreased* baking sheet. Bake in a preheated 375° oven for 8 to 12 minutes.

YIELD: 5 DOZEN

Stuffed Monkeys ·

¼ cup butter, softened

½ cup sugar

1 egg, beaten

1 cup flour

1 teaspoon baking powder

¼ teaspoon salt

1 cup chopped dates

1 cup chopped walnuts

Sugar

Cream butter and ½ cup sugar until light and fluffy; add egg. Sift together flour, baking powder, and salt; blend well with creamed mixture. Stir in dates and walnuts. Shape dough into 1-inch balls, roll in sugar, and place on a greased baking sheet. Bake in a pre-heated 375° oven for 10 minutes.

YIELD: 3 DOZEN

This old Australian recipe, circa 1850, is a sweet recollection of the past.

Dipped Gingersnaps ·

2 cups sugar

1½ cups vegetable oil

2 eggs

½ cup molasses

4 cups flour

4 teaspoons baking soda

1 tablespoons ginger

2 teaspoons cinnamon

1 teaspoon salt

Sugar

VANILLA DIP

4 cups premium white
    baking chips

¼ cup butter

Combine 2 cups sugar and oil; mix well. Add eggs, one at a time, beating well after each addition. Stir in molasses. Sift together flour, baking soda, ginger, cinnamon, and salt; gradually add to creamed mixture, blending well. Shape dough into ¾-inch balls, roll in sugar, and place 2 inches apart on an *ungreased* baking sheet. Bake in a preheated 350° oven for 10 to 12 minutes, or until cookie springs back when touched lightly. Remove to wire racks and cool.

To prepare the dip, carefully melt chips and butter in a small saucepan over very low heat. Dip cooled cookies halfway into melted mixture, shaking off excess. Place on baking sheets lined with waxed paper to harden.

YIELD: 6 DOZEN

With a distinct fragrance and pungent flavor, ginger was popular in England, and the English brought the taste with them to the New World.

Friendship Gingersnaps ·

¾ cup butter, softened

1 cup sugar

¼ cup molasses

1 egg, beaten

2 cups flour

2 teaspoons baking soda

¼ teaspoon salt

1 teaspoon cinnamon

1 teaspoon ginger

Sugar

Cream butter and 1 cup sugar; beat in molasses and egg. Sift together flour, baking soda, salt, and spices. Add dry ingredients to creamed mixture and beat well. Chill. Form dough into 1-inch balls, roll in sugar, and place on a greased baking sheet. Bake in a preheated 325° oven for 15 minutes.

YIELD: 5 DOZEN

These crisp gingersnaps, served at the governor's mansion in Connecticut around 1950, are distinguished by the robust flavor of molasses combined with spices.

Raisin Ginger Cookies · · · · · · · · · · · · · · · · · ·

¾ cup butter, softened

1 cup sugar

1 egg

¼ cup molasses

2¼ cups flour

1 teaspoon salt

2 teaspoons baking soda

¼ teaspoon cloves

1 teaspoon ginger

½ teaspoon cinnamon

1½ cups raisins

Sugar

Cream butter and 1 cup sugar; add egg. Add molasses and continue creaming until well blended. Sift together flour, salt, baking soda, and spices; add to creamed mixture and blend well. Stir in raisins. Chill dough until firm enough to handle. Shape into 1-inch balls, roll in sugar, and place on a lightly greased baking sheet. Bake in a preheated 375° oven for 8 to 10 minutes.

YIELD: 3 DOZEN

Ginger Rounds · · · · · · · · · · · · · · · · · ·

1 cup flour

1 teaspoon baking soda

¼ teaspoon salt

½ teaspoon cinnamon

1 teaspoon ginger

¼ teaspoon cloves

¼ teaspoon allspice

⅛ teaspoon black pepper

6 tablespoons butter, softened

½ cup brown sugar, packed

1 egg

2 tablespoons molasses

1 tablespoon grated lemon
 peel

1 tablespoon grated orange
 peel

Sugar

Sift together flour, baking soda, salt, and spices; set aside. Cream butter and brown sugar; add egg and molasses and continue creaming. Add grated peels and dry ingredients. Chill dough for 4 hours. Form into ½-inch balls, roll in sugar, and place on a well greased baking sheet. Bake in a 350° oven for 10 minutes.

YIELD: 5 DOZEN

OPPOSITE: Fan with painted paper leaf
England or the Netherlands, 1750s

Refrigerator Cookies

To make refrigerator cookies, form a rich dough into smooth, compact rolls. To create decorative borders, coat the outside surfaces of the prepared rolls in grated chocolate, flaked coconut, finely chopped nuts, or colored sugars. Wrap the rolls tightly in waxed paper and chill thoroughly. When you are ready to bake, slice the dough with a sharp, thin knife in a sawing motion, using as little pressure as possible. Keep the knife wiped clean.

Anise Wafers

2½ cups flour

½ teaspoon salt

1 cup butter, softened

3 ounces cream cheese, softened

1 cup sugar

1 egg yolk

½ teaspoon vanilla

2 teaspoons anise seeds

Sift together flour and salt; set aside. Cream together butter, cream cheese, and sugar until light and fluffy. Add egg yolk, vanilla, and anise seeds; beat well. Stir in dry ingredients, blending well. Shape dough into two rolls 1½ inches in diameter and wrap in waxed paper. Chill for 4 hours. Cut into ⅛-inch slices and place on an *ungreased* baking sheet. Bake in a preheated 350° oven for 10 to 12 minutes.

YIELD: 6 DOZEN

Nut Shortbread

1 cup butter, softened

⅔ cup confectioners' sugar

1½ cups flour

1 cup finely chopped pecans or skinned hazelnuts, lightly toasted

⅛ teaspoon salt

Cream butter with sugar. Stir in flour, nuts, and salt. Chill dough until firm enough to handle. Form into two 7-inch rolls and wrap in waxed paper. Chill rolls overnight. Slice into ¼-inch slices; arrange 2 inches apart on an *ungreased* baking sheet. Bake in a preheated 375° oven for 12 to 15 minutes, or until edges are golden.

YIELD: 5 DOZEN

For directions to remove skins, see Hazelnut Biscotti with Black Pepper (page 172).

Coconut Cookies ·

3⅓ cups flour

2 teaspoons baking powder

⅛ teaspoon salt

1 cup butter, melted

⅔ cup sugar

⅓ cup brown sugar, packed

2 eggs, slightly beaten

2⅓ cups flaked coconut, chopped

Sift together flour, baking powder, and salt; set aside. Cream butter with sugars. Add beaten eggs and cream until smooth and thickened. Stir in flour mixture and coconut; blend well. Form dough into two 10-inch oblongs and wrap in waxed paper. Chill thoroughly. Cut into ⅛-inch slices and place on an *ungreased* baking sheet. Bake in a preheated 400° oven for 5 to 10 minutes.

YIELD: 4 DOZEN

Serve some of these cookies as plain coconut biscuits; decorate the rest with pastel-tinted icing and sprinkle with flaked coconut.

Almond Slices ·

2¼ cups flour

1 teaspoon baking soda

1 teaspoon salt

1 cup butter, softened

1 cup brown sugar, packed

1 teaspoon almond extract

2 eggs, beaten

1 egg, lightly beaten

1 tablespoon water

30 whole blanched almonds

Sift together flour, baking soda, and salt; set aside. Cream butter, sugar, and almond extract for about 5 minutes. Add 2 eggs, stir in dry ingredients, and mix until dough forms a smooth ball. Transfer dough onto a lightly floured surface. Divide the dough into two equal portions and form two rolls. Wrap in waxed paper and chill thoroughly until firm. Cut each roll into 15 slices and place on a greased baking sheet. Slightly flatten the outer edge of each round with your hand. Gently press an almond in the center of each cookie. Mix 1 egg with water and lightly brush cookies with glaze. Bake in a preheated 350° oven for 10 to 12 minutes, or until puffed and golden brown. Cool.

YIELD: 2½ DOZEN

Javanese Shortbread

1 cup unsalted butter, softened
¾ cup sugar
1 cup flaked coconut
2 cups flour
Confectioners' sugar

Cream butter and sugar thoroughly. Add coconut and flour; mix only until blended. Chill dough until stiff enough to handle, form into rolls 1 ½ inches in diameter, and wrap in waxed paper. Chill rolls until firm. Cut into ¼-inch slices. Bake on an *ungreased* baking sheet in a preheated 300° oven for 20 to 30 minutes, or until pale on top and golden brown on the bottom. Cool for 2 minutes before removing from baking sheet. Dust generously with confectioners' sugar. Store in airtight container.

YIELD: 5 DOZEN

Sugarless Spice Cookies

½ cup butter, softened
½ cup molasses
1 egg, beaten
2½ cups flour
½ teaspoon baking powder
½ teaspoon baking soda
¼ teaspoon salt
¼ teaspoon ginger
¼ teaspoon cinnamon
¼ teaspoon allspice

Cream butter until light. Add molasses and egg; beat thoroughly. Sift together flour, baking powder, baking soda, salt, and spices. Add dry ingredients gradually to creamed mixture. Form dough into rolls 1½ inches in diameter, wrap in waxed paper, and chill overnight. Cut into ⅛-inch slices and place on a lightly greased baking sheet. Bake in preheated 375° oven for 5 to 7 minutes, or just until set.

YIELD: 6 DOZEN

Overbaking will cause cookies made without sugar to taste bitter.

Fresh Ginger Cookies ·

½ cup blanched almonds

1½ cups flour

⅛ teaspoon cloves

¼ teaspoon ground ginger

½ teaspoon cinnamon

⅛ teaspoon nutmeg

½ teaspoon baking soda

¼ teaspoon salt

2 tablespoons peeled minced
    ginger

½ cup unsalted butter, cut
    into eighths and softened

½ cup dark brown sugar,
    packed

1 egg

2 tablespoons molasses

Using a food processor, chop almonds with ½ cup flour; mix in remaining 1 cup flour, cloves, ground ginger, cinnamon, nutmeg, baking soda, and salt. Transfer to waxed paper. Place minced fresh ginger, butter, and sugar into the food processor and pulse until smooth. Add egg and molasses; process to mix. Add flour mixture and combine thoroughly. Shape into a 1 × 14-inch roll, wrap in waxed paper, and chill overnight. Slice thinly and place on a lightly greased baking sheet. Bake in a preheated 350° oven for 8 to 10 minutes.

YIELD: 12 DOZEN

Cardamom Thins ·

¾ cup butter, softened

⅔ cup brown sugar, packed

¼ cup light cream

1½ cups flour

½ teaspoon baking soda

½ teaspoon salt

2 teaspoons cardamom

Cream butter and sugar; beat in the cream. Sift together flour, baking soda, salt, and cardamom; add to creamed mixture. Chill dough until firm enough to handle. Form into a 10-inch roll, wrap in waxed paper, and chill overnight. Cut into ¼-inch slices and arrange 2 inches apart on an *ungreased* baking sheet. Bake in a preheated 375° oven for 6 to 8 minutes.

YIELD: 3½ DOZEN

Caraway Crisps

¾ cup butter, softened
½ cup brown sugar, packed
½ cup sugar
⅓ cup sour cream
1 teaspoon grated lemon peel
2 cups flour
½ teaspoon baking soda
¼ teaspoon salt
2 teaspoons caraway seeds

Cream butter and sugars. Beat in sour cream and lemon peel. Sift together flour, baking soda, and salt; add to creamed mixture. Stir in caraway seeds. Chill dough until firm enough to handle. Form into a 12-inch roll; chill for 4 hours. Cut into ¼-inch slices and arrange 2 inches apart on an *ungreased* baking sheet. Bake in a preheated 375° oven for 6 to 8 minutes.

YIELD: 4 DOZEN

Icebox Oatmeal Cookies

1 cup butter, softened
1 cup sugar
1 cup brown sugar, packed
2 eggs, beaten
1 teaspoon vanilla
1½ cups flour
1 teaspoon salt
1 teaspoon baking soda
3 cups quick oatmeal
½ cup chopped nuts

Cream butter and sugars until light and fluffy. Add eggs and vanilla. Sift together flour, salt, and baking soda. Add to creamed mixture; blend well. Add oatmeal and nuts. Shape into rolls 1½ inches in diameter, wrap in waxed paper, and chill overnight. Cut into ¼-inch slices and place on an *ungreased* baking sheet. Bake in a preheated 350° oven for 10 minutes.

YIELD: 6 DOZEN

Peanut Cookies

1 cup salted peanuts

½ cup unsalted butter, cut into
    eighths and softened

¾ cup brown sugar, packed

1 egg

2 teaspoons vanilla

1½ cups flour

½ teaspoon salt

In a food processor, chop ½ cup peanuts until the mixture looks like peanut butter. Add butter and sugar; process until smooth. Add egg and vanilla; process to mix well. Add remaining ½ cup peanuts, flour, and salt. Pulse four times, or until peanuts are chopped. Form the dough into two 7 × 2-inch rolls; wrap well in waxed paper and chill overnight. Slice thinly and arrange on a lightly greased baking sheet. Bake in a preheated 350° oven for 8 to 10 minutes.

YIELD: 8 DOZEN

Crispy Pistachio Cookies

½ cup butter, softened

1 cup sugar

1 egg

½ teaspoon almond extract

½ teaspoon grated orange peel

1½ cups flour

½ teaspoon baking powder

½ teaspoon salt

½ cup shelled, chopped
    pistachios

Cream butter and sugar until light and fluffy. Add egg, almond extract, and orange peel; beat until smooth. Sift together flour, baking powder, and salt; combine with creamed mixture. Stir in pistachios. Chill dough until firm enough to handle. Shape into a roll 2 inches in diameter; wrap in waxed paper and chill thoroughly. Cut into ¼-inch slices and place on an *ungreased* baking sheet. Bake in a preheated 400° oven for 6 to 8 minutes, or until golden brown. Cool on rack.

YIELD: 4½ DOZEN

Apple Cider Cookies ·

½ cup unsalted butter,
  softened
4 ounces cream cheese,
  softened
½ cup sugar
1 tablespoon apple cider
  or Calvados
1 egg yolk
1¾ cups flour
¼ teaspoon baking powder
¼ teaspoon baking soda
⅛ teaspoon salt
½ cup dried apples,
  chopped fine
Sugar

Cream butter, cream cheese, and ½ cup sugar; add apple cider and egg yolk, beating until smooth. Sift together flour, baking powder, baking soda, and salt; combine dry ingredients with creamed mixture. Add the apples and mix. On a piece of waxed paper, form the dough into a roll 1½ inches in diameter. Sprinkle the roll with sugar, rolling to coat it thoroughly. Wrap in waxed paper and chill for 4 hours. Cut into ⅜-inch slices and place 1 inch apart on an *ungreased* baking sheet. Bake in a preheated 350° oven for 10 to 12 minutes.

YIELD: 5 DOZEN

Lemon Tangs ·

¾ cup unsalted butter,
  softened
1 cup sugar
1 teaspoon vanilla
1½ tablespoons grated
  lemon peel
¼ cup fresh lemon juice
2¼ cups flour
1½ teaspoons baking powder
½ teaspoon baking soda
¼ teaspoon salt
Confectioners' sugar

Cream butter and sugar until light and fluffy. Add vanilla, lemon peel, and juice; beat until smooth. Sift flour with baking powder, baking soda, and salt; add to creamed mixture and blend well. Chill dough for 1 hour. Using waxed paper, form dough into rolls 1½ inches in diameter. Chill rolls overnight. Cut into slices ⅛-inch thick and place on an *ungreased* baking sheet. Bake in a preheated 350° oven for 8 minutes, or until edges are golden brown. Cool on racks and sprinkle tops with confectioners' sugar.

YIELD: 4 DOZEN

Lemon Thyme Cookies ·

1 cup butter, softened

2 cups flour

1½ cups sugar

½ teaspoon salt

½ teaspoon baking powder

grated peel of 1 lemon

¼ cup fresh thyme leaves
   or lemon thyme leaves or
   2 tablespoons dried thyme

In a large mixing bowl, beat butter, flour, ½ cup sugar, salt, and baking powder until well blended. Divide dough in half and form two cylinders, each about 1½ inches in diameter. Combine remaining 1 cup sugar, lemon peel, and thyme in a food processor or blender. Process mixture until thyme leaves are as fine as pepper. Sprinkle half the sugar mixture onto a piece of wax paper slightly longer than the length of a cylinder. Roll cylinder in sugar mixture and wrap in the waxed paper. Repeat with the second cylinder. Refrigerate until dough is firm. Cut into ⅜-inch slices; arrange on a baking sheet lined with parchment paper. Bake in a preheated 325° oven for 20 minutes, or until cookies just start to brown.

YIELD: 5 DOZEN

Lemon Nut Cookies ·

1 cup butter, softened

½ cup brown sugar, packed

½ cup sugar

1 egg, beaten

1 tablespoon fresh lemon juice

1 tablespoon grated lemon
   peel

2 cups flour

¼ teaspoon baking soda

¼ teaspoon salt

½ cup ground walnuts

Cream butter. Add sugars, egg, lemon juice, and peel; mix well. Sift flour with baking soda and salt; add nuts and stir until blended. Form dough into rolls 2 inches in diameter, wrap in waxed paper, and chill overnight. Slice thinly and place on an *ungreased* baking sheet. Bake in a preheated 375° oven for 5 to 8 minutes.

YIELD: 5 DOZEN

Orange Apricot Cookies ·

Peel of 1 small orange

½ cup dried apricots

1½ cups flour

½ cup unsalted butter, cut into
    eighths and softened

¾ cup brown sugar, packed

1 egg

1 teaspoon vanilla

¼ teaspoon salt

Remove orange peel with swivel-bladed peeler, carefully omitting any white pith. In a food processor, finely chop orange peel and apricots with ½ cup flour; set aside. Process butter, sugar, egg, and vanilla. Add fruit mixture, remaining 1 cup flour, and salt; combine thoroughly. Shape dough into two 9-inch rolls and chill until firm. Slice thinly and place 1 inch apart on a greased baking sheet. Bake in a preheated 350° oven for 8 to 10 minutes.

YIELD: 7 DOZEN

Rolled Cookies

The dough for rolled cookies is stiff enough to be spread out smoothly with a rolling pin. The dough is usually chilled before rolling, so that it will be easier to handle without the addition of too much flour. Before baking, cut the dough into desired shapes. Plan to cut cookies close together, leaving as little dough as possible to reroll. Dip a cookie cutter into flour, shake off the excess, press into the dough, and lift the cut dough onto a prepared baking sheet. Set aside all trimmings and roll separately; these cookies will be less tender because of the extra flour and handling.

Cinnamon Roll-ups

1 cup butter, softened

2 cups flour

1 egg yolk

¾ cup sour cream

¾ cup sugar

¾ cup finely chopped nuts

1 teaspoon cinnamon

1 egg white, slightly beaten

1 tablespoon water

Cut butter into flour until mixture resembles coarse crumbs. Stir in egg yolk and sour cream; mix. Chill dough for 1 to 2 hours. Combine sugar, nuts, and cinnamon. Divide dough into quarters. Roll each quarter into an 11-inch circle on a floured surface. Sprinkle with one-fourth of the nut-sugar mixture. Cut into 16 wedges. Roll up, starting at widest end. Place rolls about 2 inches apart on an *ungreased* baking sheet. Brush with combined egg white and water. Bake in preheated 350° oven for 20 minutes, or until golden brown.

Filling Variation: Combine ½ cup mini chocolate chips with sugar, nuts, and cinnamon.

YIELD: 5 DOZEN

Based on an Eastern European recipe, these popular, tender cookies have a delicious not-too-sweet filling.

OPPOSITE: Servant statue of woman grinding grain
Egypt, Old Kingdom, Dynasty 5, 2524–2400 B.C.

WALTER CRANE
Polly Put the Kettle On, 1899

German Sand Tarts

1 cup butter, softened
1¼ cups sugar
2 cups flour
1 egg, beaten
1 egg white
1 tablespoon sugar
¼ teaspoon cinnamon
30 pecan halves

Cream butter and sugar. Add flour slowly, working it in as for pastry. Add beaten egg and mix well. Chill thoroughly. Roll to ⅛-inch thickness; cut rounds and place on a lightly greased baking sheet. Beat egg white until frothy and brush on cookies. Sprinkle with sugar and cinnamon. Place pecan half firmly in the center of each cookie. Bake in a preheated 375° oven for 8 to 12 minutes.

YIELD: 2½ DOZEN

Sugar Cookies

1 cup butter
4 cups flour
1 ½ cups sugar
½ teaspoon salt
1 teaspoon baking soda
2 eggs, beaten
¼ cup milk
1 teaspoon vanilla

Cut butter into flour; add sugar, salt, and soda. Mix in eggs, milk, and vanilla. The dough handles easily and does not need to be chilled before rolling. Roll to ⅛-inch thickness and cut into various shapes. If desired, brush cookies with milk and sprinkle with sugar before baking, or frost and decorate them when cool. Bake on a greased baking sheet in a preheated 350° oven for 8 to 10 minutes.

YIELD: 7 DOZEN

This is a great holiday cookie. Use all the cookie cutters in your collection. To create edible decorations, with a drinking straw pierce a hole near the top of each cookie. When you remove the cookies from the oven, you may have to pierce the hole again. Thread ribbons through the holes of the decorated cookies.

Thin Buttery Sugar Cookies

⅔ cup unsalted butter,
    softened
¾ cup sugar
2 eggs
1 teaspoon vanilla
1 teaspoon grated lemon peel
    or orange peel
2 cups flour
¼ teaspoon salt
Cinnamon sugar or colored
    sprinkles

Cream butter and sugar until light and creamy. Add 1 egg; separate remaining egg and add yolk. Stir in vanilla and lemon peel; beat well. Gradually stir in flour and salt; blend well. Chill dough for 1 hour. On a well-floured surface, roll small amounts of dough at a time. Roll very thin; use a spatula to keep underside of dough free. Cut into fancy shapes; carefully transfer to a lightly greased baking sheet. Brush cutouts with remaining egg white; sprinkle with cinnamon sugar *or* colored sprinkles. Bake in a preheated 350° oven for 5 to 8 minutes. Watch carefully, because cookies brown quickly.

YIELD: 3 DOZEN

Crisp Molasses Cookies

½ cup butter, melted
1 cup molasses, heated
½ cup brown sugar, packed
¼ teaspoon nutmeg
¾ teaspoon ginger
¾ teaspoon cloves
¾ teaspoon cinnamon
¼ teaspoon allspice
¼ teaspoon salt
1 teaspoon baking soda
3 cups flour

Combine butter, molasses, sugar, spices, salt, and soda. Add flour and mix thoroughly. Form into a ball, wrap in plastic wrap, and chill 1 hour. Roll to ⅛-inch thickness and cut into desired shapes. Place cookies on an *ungreased* baking sheet and bake in a preheated 375° oven for 7 to 8 minutes.

YIELD: 5 DOZEN

Springerle ·

4 eggs

1 lb. confectioners' sugar

6 tablespoons butter, melted

Grated peel of 1 lemon

1 teaspoon anise oil

2 to 3 teaspoons anise seeds

4 cups flour

2 teaspoons baking powder

½ teaspoon salt

Stir eggs and sugar together, beating well for ½ hour with electric mixer. Add butter, lemon peel, anise oil, and anise seeds. Sift together flour, baking powder, and salt. Combine all ingredients and mix well. Roll dough to ½-inch thickness on a lightly floured surface. Then roll with a floured springerle rolling pin. Cut cookies apart so that each has a design. Generously grease a baking sheet, transfer cookies printed side up, and allow to stand uncovered at room temperature overnight. Bake in a preheated 325° oven for 10 to 15 minutes, or until pale gold. Cool on rack.

YIELD: 4 TO 5 DOZEN

These distinctive German anise-flavored cookies usually have embossed designs that have been imprinted either with a carved wooden rolling pin or with wooden molds. The texture and flavor improve if the cookies are allowed to age in an airtight container for a week.

Sugar box
Made by JOHN CONEY, 1655/56–1722

A perfect cake has an irresistible, ageless appeal; it creates a superb centerpiece for a tea buffet. A slice goes a long way! The secret to success is in thoroughly creaming the butter and sugar and then, after adding the eggs, beating until the mixture is pale yellow and smooth. This last beating incorporates air into the batter and thus lightens the cake.

Cakes

Teapot
China (for export), about 1770

To present a cake as dazzling in design as it is in taste:

- Crown a tender cake with creamy swirls of frosting; for additional decoration, press chopped nuts or shredded coconut onto sides of frosted cake.
- Keep the top of the cake simple yet distinctive with a stenciled design of sifted confectioners' sugar, or pipe frosting to outline the cake and then garnish with seasonal fruit.
- Create a romantic look with an assortment of fresh edible flowers, such as violets and pansies, or with fanciful curls of white or dark chocolate on top of a frosted cake.

Pumpkin Cake Roll

3 eggs
1 cup sugar
⅔ cup canned pumpkin
1 teaspoon lemon juice
¾ cup flour
1 teaspoon baking powder
½ teaspoon salt
2 teaspoons cinnamon
1 teaspoon ginger
½ teaspoon nutmeg
1 cup finely chopped walnuts
Sugar

CREAM CHEESE FILLING
1 cup confectioners' sugar
6 ounces cream cheese
4 tablespoons butter, softened
½ teaspoon vanilla

Beat eggs on high speed for 5 minutes. Gradually beat in 1 cup sugar. Stir in pumpkin and lemon juice. Sift together flour, baking powder, salt, cinnamon, ginger, and nutmeg; fold into batter. Line a greased 15 × 10 × 1-inch pan with waxed paper and grease the paper. Spread batter evenly in pan. Sprinkle with walnuts. Bake in a preheated 375° oven for 12 to 15 minutes, or until a tester inserted in the center comes out clean. Turn onto a towel sprinkled with sugar. Remove paper. Starting at wide end, roll up towel and cake together. Cool.

To make the filling, beat confectioners' sugar with cream cheese, butter, and vanilla. Unroll cake and spread with filling. Roll the cake again, wrap in foil, and chill or freeze until ready to use.

Place this impressive cake seam side down on a tray. Just before serving, dust cake with confectioners' sugar and cut crosswise into slices.

Sherry Zucchini Cake ·

2 cups grated zucchini

1 teaspoon salt

3 cups flour

1 teaspoon baking powder

1½ teaspoons baking soda

½ teaspoon salt

2 teaspoons cinnamon

1 cup vegetable oil

2 cups sugar

3 eggs

2 teaspoons vanilla

2 tablespoons sherry

1 teaspoon grated lemon peel

1½ cups chopped nuts

1 cup raisins or chopped dates

VANILLA GLAZE

1½ cups confectioners' sugar

⅛ teaspoon salt

1 tablespoon butter, softened

2 tablespoons cream or sherry

Mix zucchini with 1 teaspoon salt in colander. Press with plate and let drain 1 hour. Squeeze out excess moisture. Sift together flour, baking powder, baking soda, salt, and cinnamon; set aside. Beat together vegetable oil and sugar; add eggs, one at a time, beating well after each addition. Add vanilla, sherry, zucchini, and lemon peel; stir to blend. Add dry ingredients, nuts, and raisins. Turn into a well greased 10-inch angel food cake pan or bundt pan. Bake in a preheated 325° oven for 60 to 75 minutes. Let stand in pan about 5 minutes. Turn out on rack to cool.

If desired, combine ingredients for glaze until smooth, and glaze cake before serving.

Carrot Nut Cake ·

¼ cup orange juice

¼ cup golden raisins, chopped

2 cups flour

1 cup brown sugar, packed

½ cup sugar

2 teaspoons baking soda

1 teaspoon salt

¼ teaspoon cloves

2 teaspoons cinnamon

1 teaspoon vanilla

4 eggs

1¼ cups vegetable oil

½ pound carrots, grated

1 cup walnuts, chopped

1 tablespoon grated orange
  peel

CREAM CHEESE FROSTING

1 tablespoon butter, softened

3 ounces cream cheese

1 teaspoon vanilla

⅛ teaspoon salt

1 cup confectioners' sugar

In a 1-quart saucepan over medium heat, heat orange juice and raisins to boiling. Reduce to low and simmer uncovered 5 minutes. Set aside. Into a large bowl, measure flour, sugars, baking soda, salt, spices, vanilla, eggs, and oil. Add raisin mixture. With mixer at low, beat ingredients just until mixed, constantly scraping bowl. Increase speed to high and beat for 4 minutes. Fold in carrots, walnuts, and orange peel. Pour into a greased 13 × 9 × 2-inch pan. Bake in a preheated 325° oven for 40 to 45 minutes, or until a tester inserted in the center comes out clean. Cool cake 10 minutes before removing from pan. If you prefer, use a greased bundt pan and increase baking time to 55 to 60 minutes.

To make frosting, cream butter, cream cheese, vanilla, and salt until soft. Add confectioners' sugar, working until blended. Frost cooled cake.

Fresh shredded carrots lend sweetness and moistness to the interesting texture of this colorful cake. It keeps well for days.

Fresh Apple Cake ·

2 cups sugar

1 cup vegetable oil

2 eggs

4 cups chopped *unpeeled* apples

3 cups flour

2 teaspoons baking soda

1 teaspoon salt

1 teaspoon cinnamon

1 cup golden raisins

1 cup dark raisins

1 cup chopped nuts

Mix sugar, oil, and eggs until thoroughly blended. Stir in apples; let stand 10 minutes. Sift together flour, baking soda, salt, and cinnamon; stir into apple mixture. Fold in all raisins and nuts. Pour into a greased bundt pan. Bake in a preheated 350° oven for 60 minutes. Remove from pan and cool on rack.

Blueberry Crumb Cake ·

2 cups flour

1½ cups sugar

¾ cup cold butter, cut in pieces

2 teaspoons baking powder

1 teaspoon salt

2 egg yolks

1 cup milk

1 teaspoon vanilla

2 egg whites, beaten stiff

2 cups fresh blueberries

2 teaspoons flour

Blend flour, sugar, and butter together with pastry blender or food processor until mixture resembles coarse meal. Remove 1 cup for topping and set aside. Add baking powder, salt, egg yolks, milk, and vanilla to crumb mixture in bowl. Mix until smooth. Fold in egg whites. Pour into a greased and floured 13 × 9 × 2-inch pan. Dust the blueberries lightly with 2 teaspoons flour and spread evenly over batter. Sprinkle reserved crumb topping over the fruit. Bake in a preheated 350° oven for 40 minutes.

A wonderful light cake that will not be made too sweet by adding a simple streusel topping.

Banana Cake · · · · · · · · · · · · · ·

½ cup unsalted butter,
  softened

1¼ cups sugar

3 eggs

1 teaspoon lime juice

1½ cups mashed ripe bananas

2 cups flour

2 teaspoons baking powder

¼ teaspoon baking soda

¼ teaspoon salt

3 tablespoons milk

LEMON FROSTING

½ cup butter, softened

3 cups confectioners' sugar

3 to 4 tablespoons lemon juice

Cream butter and sugar slowly, beating well. Add eggs one at a time, beating after each addition. Add lime juice; fold in banana. Sift together flour, baking powder, baking soda, and salt; add dry ingredients alternately with milk. Spread batter evenly in a well greased bundt pan. Bake in a preheated 350° oven for 50 to 60 minutes, or until a tester inserted in the center comes out clean. Cool 10 minutes; then invert onto platter. If you prefer, use *two* well greased and floured 9-inch round cake pans and bake for 25 to 30 minutes.

To make frosting, cream butter until light and fluffy. Add confectioners' sugar; blend well. Beat in lemon juice, a tablespoon at a time, until smooth and easy to spread. Spread on cooled cake.

Yogurt Pound Cake · · · · · · · · · · · · ·

1 cup butter, softened

1½ cups sugar

3 eggs

1 teaspoon grated lemon peel

2¼ cups flour

½ teaspoon baking soda

½ teaspoon salt

1 teaspoon vanilla

1 cup orange or peach yogurt

Cream butter and sugar, add eggs and lemon peel, and mix well. Sift together flour, baking soda, and salt; add alternately with vanilla and yogurt. Pour batter into a well greased and floured bundt or tube pan. Bake in a preheated 325° oven for 60 to 70 minutes, or until a tester inserted in the center comes out clean.

Yogurt makes this cake moist and light; it is much lower in fat than one made with sour cream.

Old Fashioned Oatmeal Cake

1¼ cups boiling water

1 cup quick oatmeal

½ cup butter, softened

1 cup brown sugar, packed

1 cup sugar

2 eggs

1½ cups flour

1 teaspoon baking soda

½ teaspoon salt

½ teaspoon cinnamon

ICING

6 tablespoons butter, softened

¾ cup brown sugar, packed

1 teaspoon vanilla

1 cup coconut

Chopped nuts, if desired

Pour water over oatmeal and let stand for 20 minutes. Cream together butter and sugars. Add eggs and mix well. Pour oatmeal over creamed mixture and blend. Sift together flour, baking soda, salt, and cinnamon; add to oatmeal mixture. Pour into a greased 13 × 9 × 2-inch pan. Bake in a preheated 350° oven for 30 to 40 minutes.

Combine icing ingredients and mix well. Spread on cake while still hot and put under broiler until brown.

Finnish Buttermilk Cake

2½ cups flour

1½ cups sugar

1 teaspoon baking powder

1½ teaspoons baking soda

¼ teaspoon salt

1 teaspoon cinnamon

½ teaspoon cloves

1½ cups buttermilk

½ cup butter, melted

Sift together flour, sugar, baking powder, baking soda, salt, and spices into a mixing bowl. Stir in buttermilk; mix well. Stir in melted butter and mix well again. Pour into a greased and sugared 9-inch tube pan. Bake in a preheated 350° oven for 1 hour.

This cake has no eggs.

Ginger Pound Cake

½ cup chopped crystallized
  ginger
2 cups sifted cake flour
1 teaspoon baking powder
¼ teaspoon salt
1 cup unsalted butter, softened
1 cup sugar
4 eggs
1 teaspoon vanilla
¼ teaspoon almond extract
¼ cup milk

In a small bowl, mix ginger with ¼ cup flour to coat. Sift together the remaining 1¾ cups flour, baking powder, and salt; set aside. Cream butter and sugar until light and fluffy. Beat in eggs, one at a time. Mix vanilla and almond extract with milk; add alternately with dry ingredients, beginning and ending with the dry ingredients. Stir to make a smooth batter. Quickly fold floured ginger into batter and spoon into a greased 9 × 5 × 3-inch loaf pan. Bake in the middle of a preheated 325° oven for 60 to 70 minutes, or until a tester inserted in the center comes out clean. Cool pan on rack for about 20 minutes; remove cake from pan and cool completely.

Bundt Kuchen

1½ cups pecan halves
2⅔ cups flour
2 teaspoons baking powder
½ teaspoon salt
1 cup butter, softened
2 cups sugar
4 eggs, separated
1 cup milk
¼ cup fresh lemon juice
2 teaspoons grated lemon peel
1 teaspoon vanilla
2 teaspoons whiskey or Grand
  Marnier (optional)

Grease and flour a bundt pan; place pecan halves in grooves around bottom and sides of pan. Sift together flour, baking powder, and salt; set aside. Cream butter and gradually add sugar, creaming thoroughly; beat in egg yolks, one at a time, until smooth. Add dry ingredients to creamed mixture alternately with milk; stir in lemon juice and grated peel, vanilla, and, if desired, whiskey. Beat egg whites until stiff, but not dry; gently fold in. Carefully spoon batter into nut-lined pan. Bake in a preheated 400° oven for 15 minutes. Reduce heat to 350° and continue baking 45 to 55 minutes longer, or until a tester inserted in the center comes out clean. Cool slightly and turn out of pan.

A large, dramatic cake decorated with sensational rows of pecans.

Almond Pound Cake ·

ALMOND CRUST

⅓ cup butter, softened

½ cup brown sugar, packed

¾ cup flour

1 cup chopped almonds

POUND CAKE

1 cup flour

½ teaspoon baking powder

¼ teaspoon salt

⅓ cup butter, softened

3 ounces cream cheese, softened

½ cup sugar

2 eggs

2 teaspoons vanilla

For the crust, cream butter with brown sugar until light and fluffy. Add flour and mix until crumbly. Stir in almonds. Pat mixture evenly over bottom and halfway up sides of a lightly greased 9 × 5 × 3-inch loaf pan. Set aside.

For the cake, sift together flour, baking powder, and salt; set aside. Cream butter and cream cheese with sugar until smooth. Blend in eggs and vanilla; add dry ingredients. Spoon batter into crust-lined pan. Bake in a preheated 350° oven for 40 to 45 minutes, or until a tester inserted in the center comes out clean. Cool on rack. Run knife between cake and pan. Invert cake onto platter. Turn cake top side up. Slice thinly.

Breton Bistro Cake ·

1¼ cups unsalted butter, softened

¾ cup sugar

1 egg

2 egg yolks

⅓ cup ground blanched almonds

2 teaspoons kirsch

1½ teaspoons vanilla

1¾ cups flour

1 egg, lightly beaten

Confectioners' sugar

Candied violets (optional)

Cream butter and sugar until light and fluffy. Beat in 1 egg and the egg yolks, one at a time, beating well after each addition. Beat in almonds, kirsch, and vanilla. Fold in flour. Spoon batter into a greased 9 × 2-inch flan pan with removable bottom; spread evenly. Brush top with beaten egg. Bake in a preheated 350° oven for about 30 minutes, or until top is golden. Cool in pan on rack. Dust lightly with confectioners' sugar; decorate with violets, if desired.

The texture and flavor improve if the cake is allowed to stand covered overnight at room temperature. This crumbly shortbreadlike cake should be arranged top side up on a platter. It can be served either plain or paired with strawberries or other fresh berries.

MARY CASSATT
Tea, 1890

Tranquility Lemon Cake ·

Plain dry breadcrumbs

3 cups *unsifted, unbleached* flour

2 teaspoons baking powder

1 cup unsalted butter, softened

2 cups sugar

4 *jumbo* eggs

3 tablespoons grated lemon
    peel, packed

1 cup milk

LEMON GLAZE

½ cup sugar

½ cup lemon juice

1 tablespoon water

Confectioners' sugar

Grease a 10-inch bundt pan liberally with butter and dust with breadcrumbs. Sift together flour and baking powder; set aside. Thoroughly cream butter and sugar; beat in eggs, one at a time, until well blended. Add lemon peel. Add dry ingredients to creamed mixture alternately with milk, ending with flour. Pour batter into prepared pan. Bake in the middle of a preheated 325° oven for 60 to 70 minutes, or until a tester inserted in the center comes out clean. Remove cake from oven, cool for 5 minutes, and invert onto cake rack.

For the glaze, dissolve sugar in lemon juice and water in a small saucepan over low heat. Brush top and sides of cake while still warm. Sprinkle lightly with confectioners' sugar. Best served the same day.

This is the kind of cake you eat slowly between sips of tea. It is traditionally served at Art in Bloom Tea.

ALFRED SISLEY
Grapes and Walnuts on a Table, 1876

Nut Cake

1 cup butter, softened

2 cups sugar

1 teaspoon lemon extract or
 1½ teaspoons vanilla

4 eggs, separated

4 cups sifted cake flour

1 cup milk

½ cup ground walnuts

Confectioners' sugar

Cream butter, add sugar, and continue beating until light and fluffy. Add lemon extract *or* vanilla and beaten egg yolks. Add flour alternately with milk. Stir in nuts. Beat egg whites until stiff but not dry, and gently fold in. Pour batter into a greased and floured 10-inch tube pan. Bake in a preheated 350° oven for 45 minutes, or until a tester inserted in the center comes out clean. Do not open oven during first 40 minutes of baking. Remove from pan, cool, and sprinkle top with confectioners' sugar.

Nut lovers will enjoy this old Czechoslovakian recipe. Garnish with seedless grapes either around the edge of the cake or cascading down the side.

Holiday Nut Cake

3½ cups flour

2 teaspoons baking powder

½ teaspoon salt

¾ cup milk

¼ cup rum or brandy

1½ cups butter, softened

2 cups sugar

6 eggs

6 cups chopped pecans or
 walnuts

Sherry

Confectioners' sugar

Sift together flour, baking powder, and salt; set aside. Combine milk with rum; set aside. Cream butter and sugar until light and fluffy. Add eggs, one at a time, beating after each addition. Add flour mixture alternately with milk mixture; blend well. Stir in nuts. Turn batter into a lightly greased and floured 10-inch tube pan. Bake in a preheated 275° oven for 2½ hours, or until a tester inserted in the center comes out clean. Cool cake in pan 30 minutes on a rack. Remove from pan. Cool completely; wrap in foil. Store in cool place several days to mellow. To serve, sprinkle with sherry and confectioners' sugar. Cut in thin slices and serve at room temperature.

Pine Nut Loaves

¾ cup blanched almonds,
    finely chopped

3 cups flour

4 teaspoons baking powder

½ teaspoon salt

2 cups heavy cream

2 teaspoons vanilla

½ teaspoon almond extract

2 cups sugar

4 eggs

¾ cup pine nuts

GLAZE

⅓ cup kirsch, warmed

⅓ cup sugar

Grease generously *two* 9 × 5 × 3-inch loaf pans and coat sides and bottom of each pan with the finely chopped almonds. Sift together flour, baking powder, and salt; set aside. Whip cream until stiff. Add vanilla, almond extract, and sugar. Beat in the eggs one at a time. Carefully fold in dry ingredients. Pour a quarter of the batter into each pan. Sprinkle each pan with 2 tablespoons of pine nuts. Cover with remaining batter. Smooth the tops and sprinkle with remaining nuts. Bake in a preheated 350° oven for 60 minutes, or until a tester inserted in the center comes out clean.

For the glaze, mix kirsch and sugar together and brush on loaves while warm. Cool in pans.

Orange Poppy Seed Cake

½ cup butter, softened

¾ cup sugar

2 eggs

½ cup sour cream

⅓ cup poppy seeds

¼ cup orange juice

1 tablespoon grated
    orange peel

1 teaspoon vanilla

1¼ cups flour

½ teaspoon baking powder

¼ teaspoon baking soda

Salt, to taste

Confectioners' sugar

Poppy seeds

Cream together butter and sugar until fluffy. Beat in eggs one at a time. Add sour cream, poppy seeds, orange juice, peel, and vanilla. Sift flour with baking powder, baking soda, and salt; add to creamed mixture, combining well. Pour batter into a greased and floured 1-quart ring mold. Bake in a preheated 350° oven for 40 minutes. Let cake stand for 5 minutes before inverting on cake rack. Cool completely. Sprinkle with confectioners' sugar and poppy seeds.

Hundred Dollar Chocolate Cake ·

4 ounces unsweetened
   chocolate, melted

½ cup butter, softened

2 cups sugar

2 eggs

2 teaspoons vanilla

2 cups flour

2 teaspoons baking powder

½ teaspoon salt

1½ cups milk

1 cup chopped nuts

FROSTING

2 ounces unsweetened
   chocolate

¼ cup butter

3 cups confectioners' sugar

¼ teaspoon salt

1 tablespoon vanilla

1 tablespoon lemon juice

¼ to ⅓ cup cream

1 cup nuts, chopped

Melt chocolate in double boiler; set aside. Cream butter and sugar until light and fluffy. Add eggs and vanilla; continue beating. Add chocolate. Sift together flour, baking powder, and salt; add alternately with milk. Fold in nuts. Pour batter into a greased 10-inch tube pan. Bake in a preheated 350° oven for 45 minutes, or until a tester inserted in the center comes out clean.

To make the frosting, melt chocolate and butter in a saucepan; remove mixture from heat and cool slightly. Add confectioners' sugar, salt, vanilla, and lemon juice; beat until smooth. Add enough cream to achieve spreading consistency. Fold in nuts. Frost cooled cake.

Short-necked lute *(pipa)*
China, Qing dynasty, 1891

ELIZABETH JOHANSSON
Eggs in a Net Bag, 1985

Angel Food Cake ·

1 cup sifted cake flour

1 cup confectioners' sugar

1½ cups egg whites (about 12),
    room temperature

1 teaspoon cream of tartar

½ teaspoon salt

1 teaspoon vanilla

1 cup sugar

Before mixing ingredients, put an *ungreased* 10 × 4-inch angel food tube pan in the oven and heat it at 400°. Sift together cake flour and confectioners' sugar five times; set aside. In a large bowl, with an electric mixer at low speed, combine egg whites with cream of tartar, salt, and vanilla until frothy. Increase speed; beat mixture until very soft peaks form when the beaters are lifted. Gradually add granulated sugar, a tablespoon at a time; beat at medium speed until all the sugar is added, whites are glossy, and soft peaks form. Gently fold dry ingredients into other mixture, about ¼ cup at a time, only until ingredients are incorporated; do not stir. Remove pan and set oven to 425°. Carefully spoon batter into the hot angel food tube pan. Gently cut through batter with a knife to remove any air pockets. Bake for 23 minutes. Top will spring back when lightly touched. Invert onto funnel until cold. (The leftover yolks may be used in Sunshine Cake, page 155.)

This moist cake, baked at a high temperature, contains no fat or leavening agents. The light texture comes from air that is incorporated in the beaten egg whites and steam that forms within the cake while baking. Cream of tartar adds stability to the mixture, and flour helps maintain the volume of the egg whites.

White Buttermilk Cake ·

2 cups sugar

½ cup butter, softened

2 unbeaten egg whites

2¾ cups sifted cake flour

1 teaspoon baking soda

½ teaspoon salt

1¾ cups buttermilk

1 teaspoon vanilla

CREAMY WHITE FROSTING

½ cup butter, softened

¼ cup cream

2 teaspoons vanilla

4 cups confectioners' sugar

Cream together sugar, butter, and egg whites. Sift together two or three times flour, baking soda, and salt. Combine buttermilk and vanilla. Add dry and liquid ingredients alternately to the creamed mixture, about a third at a time. Pour into *two* round 9-inch greased pans or one 13 × 9 × 2-inch pan. Bake in a preheated 350° oven for 25 to 30 minutes. Cool.

To make the frosting, put butter, cream, and vanilla in bowl; add confectioners' sugar, one cup at a time. Beat until smooth and shiny. Spread between layers and over cake.

Buttermilk makes the difference in this delectable cake.

Basic Sponge Cake ·

6 eggs, separated

½ teaspoon cream of tartar

1½ cups sugar

1 teaspoon grated lemon peel

1 teaspoon lemon extract

1½ cups sifted cake flour

1 teaspoon baking powder

½ teaspoon salt

6 tablespoons cold water

Beat egg whites with cream of tartar until soft peaks form. Set aside. Beat egg yolks for 5 minutes. Gradually add sugar and beat until pale yellow. Add lemon peel and extract. Sift together flour, baking powder, and salt; add alternately to yolk mixture with water. Fold egg whites into yolk mixture. Pour into an *ungreased* 9-inch tube pan. Bake in a preheated 350° oven for 50 to 60 minutes. The cake is done if it springs back when pressed lightly with finger. Invert onto cake rack. Cool completely before removing from pan. Loosen sides of cake with spatula to release from pan.

This cake uses no butter; it is made instead with whole eggs, separated and whipped to maximum volume. Thoroughly beating the eggs creates a light and springy cake.

Sunshine Cake ·

11 egg yolks

2 cups sugar

½ teaspoon salt

2 teaspoons vanilla

6 tablespoons butter

1 cup milk, heated to boiling

2 cups sifted cake flour

2 teaspoons baking powder

Beat egg yolks until thick and pale yellow. Add sugar gradually; mix in salt and vanilla. Beat thoroughly. Melt butter in hot milk and slowly add to egg mixture while beating constantly. Sift together flour and baking powder; quickly beat dry ingredients into egg mixture. Line bottoms of *three* greased and floured 8-inch round layer pans. Bake in a preheated 350° oven for 25 to 30 minutes. Cool on rack for 10 minutes before removing from pans. If you prefer, use a greased and floured 10-inch tube pan; bake for 60 to 75 minutes. (Egg whites may be used in Angel Food Cake, page 153, or in meringue recipes for Drop Cookies.)

Egg whites will keep in an airtight container for one week in the refrigerator or up to six months in the freezer. Egg yolks can be frozen for up to six months; just before freezing, add ⅛ teaspoon salt for every four yolks.

Teapot in the form of
a camel
England (Staffordshire),
about 1740

Every thoughtfully prepared tea table has its own distinctive and gracious appeal. This miscellaneous collection of superb specialties contains a few surprises, provides delightful variety, and satisfies the desire for contrast.

Potpourri

Teapot
England (Longton Hall), about 1755

Tangy Bourbon Mixed Nuts

1 pound unsalted assorted nuts
¼ cup bourbon
½ cup sugar
½ teaspoon Angostura bitters
1 tablespoon Worcestershire
   sauce
1 tablespoon corn oil
½ teaspoon cayenne pepper
½ teaspoon salt
¼ teaspoon freshly ground
   black pepper
1 teaspoon cumin

Drop nuts into boiling water to cover and cook 1 minute. Drain and set aside. In a small saucepan; bring bourbon to a boil and reduce until 3 tablespoons remain. In a bowl, combine the bourbon and sugar; stir. Add the bitters, Worcestershire sauce, and corn oil. Stir in the nuts, mixing thoroughly. Let sit for 10 minutes. Spread the nuts in a jellyroll pan. Bake in a preheated 325° oven for 35 minutes, stirring every 10 minutes until liquid is absorbed. In a bowl, toss hot nuts with the cayenne pepper, salt, black pepper, and cumin; mix well. Return nuts to baking sheet and let stand until cool and dry. Store in a tightly covered container.

YIELD: 4 CUPS

Glazed Pecans

½ cup butter
2 egg whites
1 cup sugar
Salt, to taste
1 pound pecan halves

Place a 15 × 10-inch jellyroll pan containing the butter into a preheated 325° oven until butter is melted. Remove pan from oven; set aside. Beat egg whites; slowly add sugar and salt and continue beating until stiff. Stir in pecans; spread mixture over melted butter. Bake for approximately 30 minutes, turning once after 10 to 15 minutes. Pecans should be lightly browned; do not allow nuts to burn. Remove from oven and turn pecans out onto waxed paper to cool.

YIELD: 4½ CUPS

English Toffee Candy

1 cup butter

1 cup sugar

⅔ cup slivered almonds

1 cup chocolate chips

1 cup chopped walnuts
  (optional)

Melt butter. Add sugar gradually, then almonds, stirring constantly until mixture reaches the hard-ball stage (265°). Spread on a large greased baking sheet. Add chocolate chips and continue spreading until chips are melted. If desired, sprinkle walnuts on top. Refrigerate until hard. Break apart and store at room temperature.

YIELD: 4 DOZEN BROKEN PIECES

Vanilla Caramels

2 cups sugar

½ cup butter

¾ cup light corn syrup

1 cup light cream

1 cup evaporated milk

1 teaspoon vanilla

1 cup chopped nuts (optional)

Combine sugar, butter, corn syrup, and cream in a large saucepan. Cook over low to medium heat, stirring frequently, until mixture comes to a full boil. Slowly stir in evaporated milk. Continue to cook, stirring very frequently, until mixture reaches the firm-ball stage (246°). Remove saucepan from heat and stir in vanilla; add nuts if desired. Pour immediately into a buttered 11 × 7-inch baking pan. Cool. Cut caramels into squares, wrapping each piece in waxed paper.

YIELD: 6 DOZEN

Pots-Pourris in the form of a snail shell
France (Sèvres), 1756–78

Simple Delights ·

Fresh white bread, very thin
   slices
Cream cheese, softened
Melted butter
Cinnamon sugar

Gently run a rolling pin over bread to make slices even thinner. Spread bread slices with cream cheese. Remove crusts. Starting at one edge roll up each slice, gently pressing so it will hold together. Cut roll into three sections. Place melted butter in a small bowl; dip pieces into butter, coating thoroughly. Roll each piece in cinnamon sugar. Place pieces seam side down on an *ungreased* baking sheet and refrigerate a few hours to firm. Bake in a preheated 350° oven for about 15 minutes, or until nicely browned. Serve warm.

YIELD: 3 PER SLICE OF BREAD;

4 DOZEN FROM SIXTEEN SLICES

Fruit Pecan Balls ·

½ cup dried apricots, coarsely
   chopped
½ cup prunes, coarsely
   chopped
¼ cup raisins, minced
3 tablespoons Cointreau
¾ teaspoon grated orange peel
¾ cup flaked coconut
¾ cup pecans, toasted and
   chopped fine
¾ cup sugar

Combine apricots, prunes, raisins, Cointreau, and orange peel. Macerate for 1 hour; chop fine in a food processor. Stir together coconut, pecans, and fruit until the mixture holds together. Shape rounded teaspoons of the mixture into balls. Roll the balls in sugar and store in an airtight container.

YIELD: 3 DOZEN

Pear and Kiwi Preserve

¾ cup peeled, cored, chopped
    pear
1½ cups peeled, chopped kiwi
4 cups sugar
3 ounces liquid fruit pectin
½ teaspoon grated lime peel
2 tablespoons lime juice

Mash pear and kiwi together in a large bowl. Stir in sugar and let stand 10 minutes. Combine the pectin, lime peel, and lime juice. Add to fruit mixture and stir for 3 minutes. Ladle at once into clean hot jars, allowing a ½-inch headspace. Seal. Let stand overnight to set. Store in refrigerator up to one month. Serve with muffins, scones, or toast.

YIELD: 5 CUPS

Chocolate Rum Drops

1 cup almond paste
1 cup confectioners' sugar
8 ounces unsweetened
    chocolate, grated
3 tablespoons rum
1 tablespoon butter, softened
1½ tablespoons cinnamon
½ cup cocoa

Mix almond paste with sugar, chocolate, rum, and butter; blend well. Form into balls and roll in a mixture of cocoa and cinnamon. Chill.

YIELD: 5 DOZEN

Ginger Balls

4 cups confectioners' sugar
½ cup butter, softened
1 egg
Salt, to taste
1⅓ cups crystallized ginger,
    cut fine
½ cup nuts, finely chopped
Vanilla wafers, finely crushed

Combine all the ingredients, except vanilla wafer crumbs, and chill until firm. Form into 1-inch balls and roll in crumbs. Refrigerate or freeze. Can be made by chopping ginger and nuts in food processor and adding remaining ingredients.

YIELD: 5 DOZEN

Cranberry Chutney ·

1 pound cranberries, picked
    over and washed
1 cup sugar
1 cup honey
½ cup water
½ cup apple cider vinegar
1 tablespoon finely chopped
    onion
½ teaspoon ginger
½ teaspoon allspice
½ cup walnuts, finely chopped

Combine all the ingredients, except walnuts, in a saucepan. Cook until cranberries pop open, about 10 minutes. Skim foam from surface. Cool. Stir in walnuts.

YIELD: 4 CUPS

This recipe is used in Chicken Salad with Cranberry Chutney (page 40). Instead of mayonnaise or mustard, use this tangy, ruby red spread on either smoked turkey and provolone or ham and Swiss cheese croissant sandwiches. The chutney may be made ahead and frozen.

Ladyfingers ·

3 eggs, separated
⅔ cup confectioners' sugar,
    divided
½ cup sifted cake flour
⅛ teaspoon salt
½ teaspoon vanilla
Confectioners' sugar

Beat egg whites until stiff, gradually beat in ⅓ cup confectioners' sugar, and set aside. Sift together flour, remaining ⅓ cup confectioners' sugar, and salt; set aside. Beat egg yolks until thick and pale yellow. Add vanilla and fold in sifted dry ingredients. Carefully fold mixture into egg whites, three tablespoons at a time; do not overmix. Form batter into finger shapes on a baking sheet lined with parchment paper. Dust with confectioners' sugar; bake in a preheated 350° oven for 10 minutes.

YIELD: 3 DOZEN

Serve plain or put together in pairs with whipped cream, custard filling, lemon curd, or softened cream cheese mixed with chopped candied ginger.

Madeleines ·

¾ cup *clarified* unsalted butter

¾ cup sugar

½ teaspoon grated lemon peel

½ teaspoon vanilla

2 eggs

1 cup flour

Confectioners' sugar

Measure 6 tablespoons clarified butter into a mixing bowl; set aside and cool. Meanwhile brush shell-shaped Madeleine molds with remaining clarified butter. Combine cooled butter with sugar, lemon peel, and vanilla; add eggs one at a time and beat until light, creamy, and tripled in volume. Fold in flour and gently blend until smooth and thick. Spoon batter into well greased molds, filling two-thirds full. Bake on middle rack in a preheated 425° oven for 8 to 10 minutes, or until cakes are golden on top and lightly browned around the edges. Remove cakes from tins as soon as baked and cool on wire racks. If necessary, loosen each cake with the tip of a thin knife. Regrease molds before second baking. Store in an airtight container at room temperature for 1 to 2 days. Dust cakes with confectioners' sugar before serving.

YIELD: 2½ DOZEN

To clarify butter, melt slowly over low heat, until milk solids and moisture separate from fat. Skim solids from the top and discard water from the bottom.

Mushroom Meringues

¾ cup egg whites, room
   temperature (about
   6 large eggs)

¼ teaspoon salt

¼ teaspoon cream of tartar

1½ cups superfine sugar or
   granulated sugar finely
   ground in food processor

¼ teaspoon almond extract

¾ teaspoon vanilla

Cocoa

6 ounces semisweet coating
   chocolate or 1 cup
   chocolate chips

In a large bowl, with mixer at high speed, beat egg whites until foamy. Beat in salt and cream of tartar. Keep beating at low to medium speed, while adding sugar gradually. Add almond and vanilla extracts; beat at high speed until stiff, about 6 to 7 minutes. Place meringue in large pastry bag fitted with a plain ½-inch diameter tip. Line *two* large baking sheets with parchment paper.

Make mushroom stems first, while meringue is firmest. To shape stems, press out meringue vertically, lifting bag upright until stems are about ½ to ¾ inch tall. Press out caps in rounds about 1 inch in diameter. Try to keep them high and puffy rather than flat. Press points on caps flat with dampened finger; then sprinkle stems and caps with cocoa shaken from a fine mesh strainer. Bake in a preheated 225° oven for 35 minutes; then lower temperature to 200° and bake 25 minutes longer, or until meringues are dry and can be easily lifted off parchment. *The objective is to dry them with as little color as possible.* Let meringues cool completely. Remove tips of stems with serrated knife. Melt chocolate and spread on flat side of mushroom cap with a small pointed spoon. Attach stem and allow chocolate to set. Crumpled foil or small round candy mold forms make fine props to support meringues as they set.

YIELD: 6 DOZEN

The meringues can be stored in airtight tins (not in the refrigerator) and served in baskets.

WILSON'S ALBANY.

Chocolate-Dipped Strawberries or Dried Apricots · · · · · · · · · · · · · ·

20 large strawberries (with
  stems attached) or 20 whole
  dried apricots
8 ounces premium brand dark
  or white chocolate

Brush berries clean; if necessary, rinse well and dry thoroughly. Chop chocolate, melt in double boiler over barely simmering water, and stir until smooth. Transfer melted chocolate to a small bowl. Holding a berry by the stem, dip the most attractive side of the berry into chocolate to cover about three-quarters of its length. Scrape underside of berry across edge of bowl to remove excess chocolate; place on a baking sheet lined with waxed paper. Refrigerate berries until set. Berries should be served the same day they are made, as moisture from a berry will cause the chocolate to separate from it.

YIELD: 20 BERRIES

Chocolate-dipped fruit is a lovely, special addition to an artfully arranged platter of small pastries or cookies. Fruit can also be used to decorate desserts such as cakes or tortes.

OPPOSITE: ANONYMOUS AMERICAN
Wilson's Albany (strawberries), 1875

Chocolate Éclairs ·

1 cup water or milk
½ cup butter
⅛ teaspoon salt
1 cup flour
4 eggs

Boil water or milk, butter, and salt; add flour all at once, stirring constantly with a wooden spoon until the paste leaves the sides of pan and forms a smooth ball. Remove mixture from heat and cool for 4 to 5 minutes before adding eggs. Add eggs, one at a time, beating thoroughly after each addition. Beat batter until thick, velvety, and shiny.

Using a pastry bag with a plain tip, make strips 1 × 4½ inches for large éclairs and ½ × 2 inches for small. Place on a lightly greased baking sheet and bake in a preheated 425° oven for 15 minutes; reduce heat to 350° and bake 15 to 20 minutes longer. Prick with sharp knife to let out steam. Turn off oven and allow large puffs to remain 15 minutes, small puffs 10 minutes, or until no beads of moisture remain on puffs. When cool, split, remove spongy center, and fill with whipped cream or custard filling. Frost tops with chocolate icing. Éclairs can be made one day ahead and kept in an airtight container before filling and frosting.

YIELD: 12 LARGE,
24 SMALL

The eggs in éclair batter act as a leavening agent, causing the puffs to rise to several times their original size during baking. If the paste is too hot when the eggs are added, they will coagulate and prevent the dough from puffing; if the paste cools too long, the eggs will not easily blend in, and the dough will be lumpy.

Cream Puffs

1 cup water or milk
½ cup butter
⅛ teaspoon salt
1 cup flour
4 eggs

To make batter, follow directions for éclairs. To form puffs, drop dough by spoonfuls onto a baking sheet 2 inches apart. Use a tablespoon for large puffs and a teaspoon for small ones. Bake until there are no beads of moisture on the puffs, about 40 minutes for large puffs. When cool, split, remove spongy center, and fill with desired filling.

YIELD: 16 LARGE,
32 SMALL, 50 PETITE

Lemon Curd

2 teaspoons cornstarch
¼ cup fresh lemon juice
6 tablespoons sugar
3 tablespoons unsalted butter,
    cut in small pieces
3 egg yolks
2 teaspoons grated lemon peel
1 egg

Dissolve cornstarch in lemon juice; set aside. Combine remaining ingredients in heavy saucepan. Whisk in lemon juice mixture. Set over medium heat and whisk until thickened and smooth, about 5 minutes. Refrigerate in a small bowl. Cover surface with waxed paper to prevent skin from forming. Lemon curd can be prepared 1 to 2 days ahead.

For Ladyfingers: Spread 2 teaspoons of lemon curd on flat side of one ladyfinger (page 163); press flat surface of another ladyfinger on curd to form sandwich.

For Small Cream Puffs: Split cream puffs (this page) in half, remove spongy center, and fill with a small amount of lemon curd.

For Tiny Tarts: Use pastry recipe for Teatime Tassies (page 175). Press dough against bottoms and sides to line minimuffin tins; prick with fork to prevent puffing while baking. Bake shells in a preheated 450° oven for 8 to 12 minutes, or until delicately browned. After 5 minutes, prick shells again if necessary. When cool, remove tart shells from pan. Fill shells with lemon curd.

YIELD: 1 CUP

Chocolate Mousse Cups ·

CUPS

2 cups premium brand
   chocolate chips
Paper baking cups
   (1⅝-inch size)
Mini-muffin pans

MOUSSE

7 ounces Toblerone milk
   chocolate, broken into
   small pieces (no substitute)
6 tablespoons boiling water
½ cup heavy cream
2 egg whites
Salt, to taste
2 tablespoons sugar
Toblerone for shaving

Melt chocolate chips in a double boiler; when smooth, spoon enough into each paper cup to cover bottom and sides completely. Place each finished cup in mini-muffin pan; refrigerate until cold and firm. Carefully peel away paper; arrange chocolate cups on a cold baking sheet and refrigerate.

For the mousse, place 7 ounces Toblerone pieces and boiling water in a small heavy saucepan over lowest heat; stir occasionally with small wire whisk until chocolate melts. Do not overheat. Small bits of almond and melting nougat *should remain*. Chill mixture in freezer, stirring occasionally, until cold enough to thicken very slightly; watch carefully so mixture does not harden. While chocolate is chilling, whip cream until it holds a definite shape; set aside. In small bowl, beat egg whites and salt to form a soft shape; gradually add sugar and continue to beat until mixture holds a firm shape. In medium bowl, fold together chocolate, beaten egg whites, and whipped cream only until incorporated. Spoon mousse into chocolate cups. Using a vegetable peeler, shave curls over tops. Freeze until ready to use.

YIELD: 3 DOZEN

OPPOSITE: JOSEPH RODEFER DECAMP
The Blue Cup, 1909

Hazelnut Biscotti with Black Pepper ·

1½ cups hazelnuts

1¾ cups unbleached flour

½ teaspoon baking powder

½ teaspoon baking soda

⅛ teaspoon salt

1½ teaspoon freshly ground
   black pepper

½ cup unsalted butter,
   softened

1 cup sugar

2 eggs

1 teaspoon finely grated
   lemon peel

1 teaspoon finely grated
   orange peel

1½ teaspoons vanilla

¼ teaspoon almond extract

Preheat oven to 300°. Place hazelnuts on a baking sheet and roast until lightly browned, about 12 minutes. Rub warm nuts in a dishtowel to remove most of the skins. Coarsely chop nuts and set aside. Sift together flour, baking powder, baking soda, salt, and pepper; set aside. In a large bowl, cream butter and sugar until light and fluffy, about 3 minutes at medium speed. Add eggs, one at a time, beating well after each addition. Beat in lemon peel, orange peel, vanilla, and almond extract. Using a rubber spatula, fold in the hazelnuts and sifted dry ingredients just until incorporated. On a lightly floured work surface, shape dough into two 12-inch logs, 3 inches wide and 1 inch thick. Place logs about 4 inches apart on a large, heavy, greased baking sheet. Bake in the middle of a 300° oven for 25 minutes, or until logs are lightly browned and feel firm when pressed in the center. The logs have a tendency to spread while baking. A large heavy knife drawn along the length of the logs, after the first few minutes of baking but before the logs have set, will help keep logs uniform. Let cool on baking sheet for 10 minutes. Carefully transfer logs to a cutting board. Using a serrated knife, cut logs crosswise into ¾-inch slices. Arrange slices cut side down on a baking sheet; bake for 7 minutes, or until golden. Turn slices; continue baking until other side is golden. Transfer to rack and cool completely. Store in an airtight tin for up to two weeks.

YIELD: 2 DOZEN

When cooled, biscotti can be dipped in melted chocolate for a fancier presentation.

Cinnamon Nut Palmiers ·

1 sheet frozen puff pastry,
  thawed

1 cup sugar

1 egg, lightly beaten

½ cup hazelnuts, finely
  chopped

2 teaspoons cinnamon

Cut puff pastry sheet in half lengthwise. Sprinkle work surface with 6 tablespoons sugar and lightly roll one piece of pastry into a 12 × 6-inch rectangle. Gently brush with beaten egg. Combine nuts, ¼ cup sugar, and cinnamon; sprinkle half the mixture evenly over pastry. Fold long edges of pastry to meet in the center; brush with beaten egg. Then fold one long side of pastry over the other, forming four layers. Using a sharp knife, cut into ½-inch slices; place 1 inch apart on a baking sheet lined with parchment paper. Chill in refrigerator for 15 minutes. Sprinkle remaining 6 tablespoons sugar on work surface and repeat folding process with other sheet of pastry. Bake in a preheated 425° oven for 10 to 12 minutes. Store in an airtight container at room temperature for 2 to 3 days.

YIELD: 3 DOZEN

These fancy puff pastry cookies resemble butterflies and have a crisp, flaky texture.

Bowl
Japan, 18th century

When the pie was open'd
The birds began to sing

WALTER CRANE

When the Pie Was Open'd the Birds Began to Sing

Teatime Tassies

PASTRY

3 ounces cream cheese, softened

½ cup butter, softened

1 cup flour

PECAN FILLING

1 egg

¾ cup brown sugar, packed

1 tablespoon butter, softened

1 teaspoon vanilla

Salt, to taste

1 cup broken pecans

To make pastry, blend together cream cheese and butter; stir in flour. Chill dough for 1 hour. Shape into 2 dozen 1-inch balls; place in *ungreased* 1¾-inch muffin pans. Press dough against bottoms and sides to form tart shells.

For the filling, beat together egg, sugar, butter, vanilla, and salt, just until smooth. Stir in pecans. Fill shells with mixture. Bake in a 325° oven for 25 minutes, or until filling is set. Cool and remove from pans.

YIELD: 2 DOZEN

Parmesan Palmiers

1 sheet frozen puff pastry, thawed

1 cup grated Parmesan cheese

1 egg, lightly beaten

¼ cup dried herbs (dill, basil, thyme, or herbes de Provence)

Cut pastry sheet in half lengthwise. Sprinkle work surface with 6 tablespoons Parmesan cheese, and lightly roll one piece of pastry into a 12 × 6-inch rectangle. Brush with beaten egg. Sprinkle 2 tablespoons Parmesan cheese and 2 tablespoons dried herbs over pastry. Fold long edges of pastry to meet in the center; brush with beaten egg. Then fold one long side of pastry over the other, forming four layers. Using a sharp knife, cut into ½-inch slices; place 1 inch apart on a baking sheet lined with parchment paper. Chill in refrigerator for 15 minutes. Bake in a preheated 425° oven for 10 to 12 minutes, or until golden. Repeat process with other half sheet of pastry. Warm before serving.

YIELD: 3 DOZEN

Herbes de Provence is a blend of five spices—thyme, basil, savory, fennel, and lavender.

Scottish Shortbread

1½ cups sifted cake flour
¼ cup cornstarch
½ cup butter, softened
⅓ cup sugar
Sugar (optional)

Sift cake flour and cornstarch together. Cream butter, gradually add sugar, and beat until light and fluffy. Add dry ingredients gradually until dough is stiff enough to work with hands. Knead in remaining dry ingredients until dough is well blended and forms a ball. Shape dough on a baking sheet into two round cakes, each about 4 inches in diameter. Using a sharp knife, deeply score each cake into eight wedges and prick surface with a fork. Edges may be fluted or pressed with tines of fork. Bake in a preheated 325° oven for 15 minutes, reduce heat to 275°, and continue baking for 30 minutes. Sprinkle with sugar, if desired, and let cool for 5 minutes before removing from baking sheet. When thoroughly cool, store in airtight container.

YIELD: 16 WEDGES

These buttery wedges are especially tender because they are made with cake flour and cornstarch.

Caraway Cheese Straws

½ cup butter
4 ounces cream cheese
1 cup flour
¼ teaspoon salt
1 egg yolk
2 teaspoons milk
½ cup grated Parmesan cheese
2 teaspoons caraway seeds

Cream butter and cream cheese; gradually blend in flour and salt. Form into ball. Chill. Divide dough in half. Roll each half into a rectangle ½-inch thick. Dilute egg yolk with milk and brush on pastry. Sprinkle with grated Parmesan cheese and caraway seeds; roll lightly with rolling pin. Cut pastry into 3 × ¾-inch strips. Place on a greased baking sheet. Bake on upper shelf at 450° for 8 to 9 minutes. Serve warm.

YIELD: 2 DOZEN

Savory Cheese Wafers

½ pound Brie or Roquefort
    cheese
½ cup cold butter
1¼ cups flour
2 teaspoons dry mustard
½ teaspoon salt
White pepper, to taste
1 egg, beaten with ½ teaspoon
    water
1 cup chopped walnuts

Remove crust of cheese. Cut cheese and butter into small pieces; place in food processor along with flour, dry mustard, salt, and pepper. Process for a few seconds until dough forms. Shape dough into two rolls about 1½ inches in diameter. Coat each roll with beaten egg, dry for a few minutes, and then roll in chopped walnuts. Wrap and chill. Cut each roll into 15 slices. Bake on an *ungreased* baking sheet in a preheated 425° oven for 12 to 15 minutes.

YIELD: 2½ DOZEN

Gougères

1 cup water
½ cup butter
¼ teaspoon salt
1 cup flour
4 eggs
¾ cup shredded sharp
    Cheddar cheese
1 to 2 tablespoons
    sesame seeds

In a medium saucepan, heat water, butter, and salt to boiling; stir in flour with wooden spoon. Cook, stirring constantly, until paste is smooth and begins to pull away from side of pan; remove from heat. Add eggs one at a time, beating well with spoon after each addition. Beat in ½ cup cheese. Drop tablespoons of dough 1 inch apart onto a greased baking sheet. Sprinkle with remaining cheese and sesame seeds. Bake in a preheated 375° oven for 25 to 35 minutes, or until puffs are firm and golden brown. Pierce top of each puff with sharp knife. Bake an additional 5 minutes. Serve warm.

YIELD: 4 DOZEN

Gougères look attractive made in the shape of a ring. Drop tablespoons of dough ½ inch apart in a circle onto a greased baking sheet. Serve ring on a platter.

HENRY SARGENT
The Tea Party, about 1824

List of Works of Art

FRONT COVER: MARY CASSATT
American, 1844–1926
The Tea (detail), 1879–80
Oil on canvas; 25½ × 36¼ in.
M. Theresa B. Hopkins Fund, 1942   42.178

BACK COVER: DOROTHY LAKE GREGORY
American, active 20th century
The Mad Teaparty
Lithograph on cream wove paper; 7⅝ × 17 in.
Gift of Mrs. Irene U. Blair, 1941   41.708

BACK COVER FLAP: SCOTT PRIOR
American, born 1949
Nanny and Rose (detail), 1983
Oil on canvas; 66 × 58 in.
Gift of the Stephen and Sybil Stone Foundation, 1984
1984.135

PAGE 1: PETER PLAMONDON
American, born 1939
Quilt with Green Teapot (detail), 1975
Oil on canvas; 43 × 46½ in.
Gift of Stephen and Sybil Stone, 1983   1983.296

PAGE 2: MARY CASSATT
American, 1844–1926
Afternoon Tea Party, 1890–91
Dry-point and aquatint in color; 13¾ × 10⅜ in.
Gift of William Emerson and the Charles Henry
Hayden Fund, 1941   41.811

PAGE 6: Tea table
Massachusetts (Boston), 1750–75
Mahogany; 27¾ × 32⅜ × 23⅜ in.
The M. and M. Karolik Collection of Eighteenth-
Century American Arts, 1941   41.592

PAGE 9: Teapot
Massachusetts, 1976
Made by DAVID DAVISON, born 1942
Porcelain; height: 13 in.
Gift of Mr. and Mrs. Stephen D. Paine, 1978
1978.501 a–b

PAGE 10 (TOP): Woman cooking
Greece (Tanagra), about 5th century B.C.
Terracotta; height: 5⅜ in.
Catharine Page Perkins Fund, 1897   97.352

PAGE 10 (BOTTOM): Woman grating cheese
Greece (Tanagra), about 5th century B.C.
Terracotta; height: 3¾ in.
Gift by contribution, 1901   01.7783

PAGE 15: Teapot with Dutch fittings
Japan, Edo period, about 1670–1700
Porcelain with overglaze enamels and silver gilt
(Kakiemon ware); height: 4 in.
Keith McLeod Fund, 1986   1986.342

PAGE 16: Tea bags
Japan, 19th century
Brocade
Gift of Denman Waldo Ross, 1915
15.621, 623, 626

Tea Jar
Japan, 16th–17th century
Imbe ware; stoneware with ivory lid; 2⅞ in.
Edward Sylvester Morse Collection, 1892   92.3373

PAGE 17: HONORÉ DAUMIER
French, 1808–1879
Le thé foin (Here you are, sir. I've brought an entire bale, sir.
Make your own tea, as strong as you like.), 1857
Lithograph; 9¼ × 11¾ in.
Bequest of William P. Babcock   B4184.50

PAGE 19: PIERRE FILLOEUL
French, 18th century
After Jean-Baptiste-Siméon Chardin, French,
1699–1779
Woman Having Tea, 1749
Engraving on dark green antique laid paper;
10⅞ × 12¼ in.
Bequest of William P. Babcock   B1471

PAGE 20: ALBERT ANDRÉ
French, 1869–1954
Woman at Tea, 1917
Oil on canvas; 20 × 23⅜ in.
Bequest of John T. Spaulding, 1948   48.517

PAGE 21: Tea caddy
Japan
Made by MIURA KENYA, Japanese, 1821–1889
Stoneware with enameled decoration; 3 × 3 in.
Edward Sylvester Morse Collection, 1892   92.6746

PAGE 22: Épergne
England (London), about 1760
Marked by JOHN PARKER and EDWARD WAKELIN,
active 1762
Silver; height: 19¾ in.
Theodora Wilbour Fund in Memory of
Charlotte Beebe Wilbour, 1965   65.915

PAGE 25: Teapot
Germany (Meissen), about 1730–35
Porcelain; height: 5⅞ in.
Gift of Mrs. Edward Pickman, 1962   62.805 a–b

PAGE 27: DOROTHY LAKE GREGORY
American, active 20th century
The Mad Teaparty
Lithograph on cream wove paper; 7⅝ × 17 in.
Gift of Mrs. Irene U. Blair, 1941   41.708

PAGE 28: PETER PLAMONDON
American, born 1939
Quilt with Green Teapot, 1975
Oil on canvas; 43 × 46½ in.
Gift of Stephen and Sybil Stone, 1983   1983.296

PAGE 30: BARNET RUBENSTEIN
American, born 1923
Oyster Pails #4, 1978–79
Oil on canvas; 40 × 52 in.
The Tompkins Collection, 1979   1979.624

PAGE 34: MAURICE BRAZIL PRENDERGAST
American (born Canada), 1858–1924
Still Life, about 1910–13
Oil on canvas; 19¼ × 21⅛ in.
Gift of Mrs. Charles Prendergast in honor of
Perry T. Rathbone, 1970   1970.1

PAGE 38: Fish plate
Italy (Campania), about 350–325 B.C.
PAINTER RELATED TO THE D'AGOSTINO PAINTER
Terracotta; diameter: 8⅞ in.
Henry Lillie Pierce Fund, 1901   01.8096

PAGE 45: Tea kettle
France (Sèvres), 1779
Porcelain; height: 7⅛ in.
Gift of Miss Charlotte Brayton, 1975   1975.658 a–b

PAGE 46: SUZUKI HARUNOBU
Japanese, 1725–1770
Ofuji Visits Osen at the Kagiya Teashop, 1769–70
Woodblock print, ink and color on paper; 11¼ × 8½ in.
William S. and John T. Spaulding Collection, 1921
21.4976

PAGE 49: MIRIAM SCHAPIRO
American, born 1923
Welcome to Our Home, 1983
Oil on fabric and canvas; 90 × 144 in.
Anonymous Gift, 1986   1986.107

PAGE 53: LUIS MELÉNDEZ
Italian (worked in Spain), 1716–1780
Still Life with Melons and Pears, about 1770
Oil on canvas; 24⅜ × 33½ in.
Margaret Curry Wyman Fund, 1939   39.40

PAGE 56: Painted shroud
Egypt, 18th Dynasty, 1570–1293 B.C.
Painted linen; 12¾ × 10 in.
William Stevenson Smith Fund, 1981   1981.657

PAGE 58: Cylinda Line teapot, coffeepot, sugar bowl, and creamer
Denmark (Copenhagen), designed in 1967
Designed by ARNE JACOBSEN, 1902–1971
Stainless steel and black nylon; height of creamer: 3¾ in.
Gift of Bloomingdale's, 1974   1974.58–62

PAGE 59: Teapot
England (London), about 1690
Silver gilt; height: 4⅝ in.
Theodora Wilbour Fund in Memory of Charlotte Beebe Wilbour, 1955   55.193 a–b

PAGE 63: Teapot
Germany (Hoechst), about 1750
Tin-glazed earthenware; height: 5½ in.
John Goelet Departmental Fund, 1968   68.714 a–b

PAGE 64: ROBERT LOUIS FRANK
American, 1924–1956
Coffee Shop, Railway Station—Indianapolis, about 1956; printed 1979
Silver print; 8⅝ × 12⅞ in.
Sophie M. Friedman Fund, 1980   1980.225

PAGE 77: LOUIS LOZOWICK
American (born Russia), 1892–1973
Still Life #2 (Still Life with Apples), 1929
Lithograph; 10⅜ × 13¼ in.
Gift of Mrs. Charles Gaston Smith's Group, 1931   31.1371

PAGE 78: JUSTE-NATHAN BOUCHER, called FRANÇOIS BOUCHER, FILS
French, 1736–1782
Plate 8 from *Cahiers d'arabesques*, 1780s
Etching; 13⅛ × 10 in.
William A. Sargent Fund, 1963   63.563

PAGE 83: Pedal harp
France (Paris), about 1785
Made by GODEFROI HOLTZMAN, French, active 1781–1794
Maple; height: 62 in.
Leslie Lindsey Mason Collection, 1918   18.30

PAGE 85: Teapot
England, about 1785
Basalt; height: 5 in.
Gift of the estate of Mrs. William Dorr Boardman through Mrs. Bernard C. Wald, 1924   24.29 a–b

PAGE 93: JOHN SINGLETON COPLEY
American, 1738–1815
Paul Revere, 1768
Oil on canvas; 35⅛ × 28½ in.
Gift of Joseph W. Revere, William B. Revere, and Edward H. R. Revere, 1930   30.781

PAGE 103: JUAN GRIS
Spanish, 1887–1927
Still Life with a Mandolin, 1925
Oil on canvas; 28¾ × 37⅞ in.
Gift of Joseph Pulitzer, Jr., 1967   67.1161

PAGE 105: Guitar
France (Paris), 1680
Made by ALEXANDRE VOBOAM, French, active 1652–1680
Yew, spruce, and ebony; inlaid with ebony and ivory; height: 36¼ in.
Otis Norcross Fund, Gift of Mr. and Mrs. Richard M. Fraser and Bequest of Gertrude T. Taft, by exchange, 1993   1993.576

PAGE 107: Teapot
England (Staffordshire), about 1750
Red stoneware; height: 4⅜ in.
Gift of Mrs. Lloyd E. Hawes, from the Collection of Lloyd E. Hawes, M.D., 1993   1993.963 a–b

PAGE 113: Sugar bowl and creampot
Massachusetts (Boston), 1761
Made by PAUL REVERE, 1735–1818
Silver; sugar bowl height: 6½ in.; creampot height: 4⅜ in.
Pauline Revere Thayer Collection, 1935   35.1781, 1782

PAGE 120: Fan with painted paper leaf
England or the Netherlands, 1750s
Skin leaf (single), painted in gouache with touches
of gilt; maximum open: 20⅝ in.
The Elizabeth Day McCormick Collection, 1943
43.2081

PAGE 130: Servant statue of woman grinding grain
Egypt, Old Kingdom, Dynasty 5, 2524–2400 B.C.
Limestone; length: 17¾ in.
Harvard University–Museum of Fine Arts
Expedition, 1921   21.2601

PAGE 132: WALTER CRANE
British, 1845–1915
Polly Put the Kettle On
Color wood engraving from *The Baby's Bouquet*,
George Routledge & Sons, London, 1899; 6 × 6 in.
Gift of Miss Ellen T. Bullard, 1956   56.884

PAGE 135: Sugar box
Massachusetts (Boston), 1680–85
Made by JOHN CONEY, 1655/56–1722
Silver; height: 4⅞ in.
Gift of Mrs. Joseph Richmond Churchill, 1913   13.421

PAGE 137: Teapot
China (for export), about 1770
Porcelain; height: 5⅞ in.
Bequest of Janet M. Wolfson, 1982   1982.99 a–b

PAGE 146: MARY CASSATT
American, 1844–1926
Tea, 1890
Drypoint; 7⅛ × 6⅛ in.
Keppel Memorial Prints. Gift of David Keppel
M25007

PAGE 148: ALFRED SISLEY
British (worked in France), 1839–1899
Grapes and Walnuts on a Table, 1876
Oil on canvas; 15 × 21⅞ in.
Bequest of John T. Spaulding, 1948   48.601

PAGE 151: Short-necked lute *(pipa)*
China, Qing dynasty, 1891
Wutong, other woods, and ivory; height: 41 in.
Leslie Lindsey Mason Collection, 1917   17.2049

PAGE 152: ELIZABETH JOHANSSON
American, born 1954
Eggs in a Net Bag, 1985
Graphite on paper; 30⅛ × 22⅜ in.
Gift of Stephen and Sybil Stone, 1986   1986.321

PAGE 155: Teapot in the form of a camel
England (Staffordshire), about 1740
Salt-glazed stoneware; height: 8⅛ in.
Gift of Mrs. George Linder, 1908   08.166 a–b

PAGE 157: Teapot
England (Longton Hall), about 1755
Porcelain; height: 5½ in.
Jessie and Sigmund Katz Collection, 1988
1988.908 a–b

PAGE 160: Pots-Pourris in the form of a snail shell
France (Sèvres), 1756–78
Porcelain; height: 5¼ in.
Bequest of Forsyth Wickes
Forsyth Wickes Collection, 1965   65.1859 a–b,
1860 a–b

PAGE 166: ANONYMOUS AMERICAN
Wilson's Albany (strawberries)
From *Nurseryman's Pocket Book of Specimen Fruit
and Flowers*, D. M. Dewey, 1875
Stencil and watercolor; 8¾ × 5⅜ in.
Gift of Mrs. Alan Tawse, 1970   1970.548

PAGE 170: JOSEPH RODEFER DECAMP
American, 1858–1923
The Blue Cup, 1909
Oil on canvas; 49⅞ × 41⅛ in.
Gift of Edwin S. Webster, Lawrence J. Webster, and
Mrs. Mary S. Sampson in Memory of their father,
Frank G. Webster, 1933   33.532

PAGE 173: Bowl
Japan, Edo period, 18th century
Takamatsu ware, stoneware with glaze; 2¾ × 4¾ in.
Edward Sylvester Morse Collection, 1892   92.4867

PAGE 174: WALTER CRANE
British, 1845–1919
When the Pie Was Open'd the Birds Began to Sing
Color wood engraving by Edmund Evans from
Sing a Song of Sixpence; 9 × 7¼ in.
Anonymous Gift

PAGE 178: HENRY SARGENT
American, 1770–1845
The Tea Party, about 1824
Oil on canvas; 64⅜ × 52⅜ in.
Gift of Mrs. Horatio A. Lamb in Memory of
Mr. and Mrs. Winthrop Sargent, 1919   19.12

PAGE 185: Tea service
France (Sèvres), 1761
Soft-paste porcelain; diameter of tray: 9 in.
Gift of Rita and Frits Markus of New York and
Chatham, Massachusetts, 1983   1983.211–218

PAGE 186: SUZUKI HARUNOBU
Japanese, 1725–1770
Deutzia: The Maid of Kasamori from the series *Popular
Beauties with Flowers*
Woodblock print, ink and color on paper;
11¼ × 8⅛ in.
Bigelow Collection. Gift of William Sturgis
Bigelow, 1911   11.19515

Acknowledgments

The Ladies Committee was founded in 1956 to promote and enhance membership in the Museum of Fine Arts, Boston. The committee strives to make the Museum a positive and enriching experience for all visitors. Its seventy members, who serve four-year terms, represent many geographical and cultural communities.

An outgrowth of the Ladies Committee, the Ladies Committee Associates was established in 1965. The committee provides the Associates an opportunity for continued interest in and service to the Museum. Membership, which is open to all who have served a minimum of two years on the Ladies Committee, currently numbers more than four hundred.

Together, these organizations created four cookbooks, all of which are out of print. Because of constant requests for those books, the Ladies Committee Associates has revised the most popular, *Boston Tea Parties,* printed in 1987. The Associates also plan to continue publishing outstanding recipes in the next millennium.

Cookbook Committee

> Judith Chamberlain
>
> Molly Dow
>
> Phyllis Katz
>
> Janet Sears Kostoff
>
> Betsy Heald
>
> Jane Hinkley
>
> Kim Hublitz
>
> Nancy McMahon
>
> Ann Schwarz
>
> Kathryn Thomas

The committee wishes to thank the members of the Ladies Committee Associates, Museum staff, and friends who generously shared the valued recipes that they contributed to the original cookbook.

The committee is further grateful to the entire Ladies Committee for underwriting this project, and for the exceptional assistance provided by members of the Ladies Committee and the Ladies Committee Associates, in particular,

Molly Batchelder and Mary-Alice Raymond for their excellent proofreading, Terry Aufranc and Marilyn MacLellan for their wise counsel, and Anne Harper for her extensive art research.

Thanks are owed to members of the Museum staff for lending their unique skills and advice: Nancy Allen, Carl Beck, Erin Bennett, Kristin Bierfelt, Jessica Blades, Carlee Bradbury, George Chamberlain, Sean Halpert, Tom Lang, Peter Littlefield, Nicole Luongo, Julia McCarthy, Patrick Murphy, Marianne Pitkin, Mark Polizzotti, Sam Quigley, Dan Reardon, Jennifer Riley, and Angela Segalla.

Tea service
France (Sèvres), 1761

Index

Almond Pound Cake, 145
Almond Slices, 123
Angel Food Cake, 153
Angel Kisses, 86
Anise Wafers, 122
Apple Cider Cookies, 128
Apricot Balls, 108
Apricot Buttons, 108
Apricot Nut Bread, 52
Bacon Filling, 41
Banana Cake, 142
Banana Nut Drops, 88
BAR COOKIES, 62
    Bourbon Pecan Bars, 71
    Brown Sugar Bars, 67
    Cheesecake Squares, 82
    Chocolate Peppermint Squares, 67
    Choco-Peanut Breakaways, 70
    Cranberry Crumbles, 74
    Date Nut Bars, 71
    English Toffee Squares, 81
    Espresso Brownies, 65
    Fresh Apple Cake Bars, 75
    Golden Apricot Bars, 75
    Golden Lemon Bars, 83
    Grand Marnier Brownies, 66
    Hermits, 79
    Holiday Lebkuchen, 80
    Honey Bars, 73
    Jon Vie Brownies, 65
    Lemon Love Bars, 82
    Linzer Bars, 68
    Nutmeg Cake Squares, 69
    Nutty Coconut Bars, 70
    Pecan Bars, 72
    Pecan Turtles, 72
    Praline Grahams, 80
    Prune Nut Bars, 76
    Pumpkin Bars, 78
    Scottish Butter Squares, 81
    Snow on the Mountain Bars, 74
    Sour Cream Apple Squares, 76
    Sour Cream Rhubarb Squares, 79

    Thin Chocolate Squares, 64
    Vienna Raspberry Chocolate Bars, 68
    White Chocolate and Macadamia Nut Blondies, 69
    Zebras, 73
Basic Sponge Cake, 154
Benne Wafers, 112
Blueberry Crumb Cake, 141
Blueberry Muffins, 54
Bourbon Drops, 102
Bourbon Pecan Bars, 71
Breton Bistro Cake, 145
Broccoli Tea Sandwiches, 43
Brown Sugar Bars, 67
Brown Sugar Cookies, 112
Brown Sugar Nut Cookies, 97
Brownie Chocolate Chip Cookies, 95
Brownie Drops, 94
Bundt Kuchen, 144
Butter Spread Sandwiches, 31
Butterhorns, 61
Buttermilk Scones, 60
Buttery Brandy Wreaths, 111
CAKES, 136
    Almond Pound Cake, 145
    Angel Food Cake, 153
    Banana Cake, 142
    Basic Sponge Cake, 154
    Blueberry Crumb Cake, 141
    Breton Bistro Cake, 145
    Bundt Kuchen, 144
    Carrot Nut Cake, 140
    Finnish Buttermilk Cake, 143
    Fresh Apple Cake, 141
    Ginger Pound Cake, 144
    Holiday Nut Cake, 149
    Hundred Dollar Chocolate Cake, 151
    Nut Cake, 149
    Old Fashioned Oatmeal Cake, 143
    Orange Poppy Seed Cake, 150
    Pine Nut Loaves, 150
    Pumpkin Cake Roll, 138
    Sherry Zucchini Cake, 139
    Sunshine Cake, 155

OPPOSITE: SUZUKI HARUNOBU
Deutzia: The Maid of Kasamori, about 1770

CAKES *(continued)*
   Tranquility Lemon Cake, 147
   White Buttermilk Cake, 154
   Yogurt Pound Cake, 142
Canapés, instructions, 26
Caraway Cheese Straws, 176
Caraway Crisps, 126
Cardamom Thins, 125
Carrot Nut Cake, 140
Carrot Raisin Filling, 43
Cheesecake Squares, 82
Chicken Pecan Sandwiches, 42
Chicken Salad with Cranberry Chutney, 40
Chive Butter, 32
Chocolate Chip Snowballs, 116
Chocolate Chocolate Chip Cookies, 97
Chocolate Crinkles, 116
Chocolate Éclairs, 168
Chocolate Fruit Drops, 94
Chocolate Lace Cookies, 104
Chocolate Meringues, 87
Chocolate Mousse Cups, 171
Chocolate Peanut Drops, 95
Chocolate Peppermint Squares, 67
Chocolate Rum Drops, 162
Chocolate-Dipped Strawberries or Dried Apricots, 167
Chocolate Walnut Wafers, 92
Choco-Peanut Breakaways, 70
Christmas Cookies, 109
Cinnamon Butter Pinwheels, 33
Cinnamon Nut Palmiers, 173
Cinnamon Roll-ups, 131
Classic Chilled Tea, 22
Closed Sandwiches, instructions, 27
Coconut Cookies, 123
Coconut Snowdrops, 86
Cookies. *See* Bar Cookies, Drop Cookies, Shaped Cookies
Crabmeat Filling, 41
Cranberry Chutney, 163
Cranberry Cookies, 91
Cranberry Crumbles, 74
Cranberry Lemon Bread, 54
Cream Cheese and Strawberry Sandwiches, 35
Cream Cheese Spread Sandwiches, 35
Cream Puffs, 169
Crisp Molasses Cookies, 134
Crisp Spice Cookies, 102
Crispy Pistachio Cookies, 127
Crunchy Pecan Cookies, 114
Cucumber Mint Filling, 43
Curry Scones with Chutney Butter, 57
Date Bacon Sandwiches, 40

Date Cashew Honeys, 92
Date Macaroons, 87
Date Nut Bars, 71
Date Nut Bread, 48
Dipped Gingersnaps, 119
DROP COOKIES, 84
   Angel Kisses, 86
   Banana Nut Drops, 88
   Bourbon Drops, 102
   Brown Sugar Nut Cookies, 97
   Brownie Chocolate Chip Cookies, 95
   Brownie Drops, 94
   Chocolate Chocolate Chip Cookies, 97
   Chocolate Fruit Drops, 94
   Chocolate Lace Cookies, 104
   Chocolate Meringues, 87
   Chocolate Peanut Drops, 95
   Chocolate Walnut Wafers, 92
   Coconut Snowdrops, 86
   Cranberry Cookies, 91
   Crisp Spice Cookies, 102
   Date Cashew Honeys, 92
   Date Macaroons, 87
   French Nut Drops, 87
   Irish Lace Cookies, 104
   Lacy Hazelnut Cookies, 105
   Lemonade Drops, 91
   Melted Moments, 101
   Michigan Rocks, 100
   Mocha Divines, 101
   Needless Markup Cookies, 96
   Orange Cookies, 90
   Peanut Butter Crinkles, 100
   Pine Nut Cookies, 99
   Pumpkin Cookies, 90
   Scottish Oat Surprises, 88
   Sesame Seed Cookies, 98
   Sleeping Macaroons, 86
   Soft Ginger Cookies, 89
   Sour Cream Cookies, 89
   Toffee Crunch Cookies, 98
   Walnut Chews, 99
   White Chocolate and Cashew Cookies, 96
English Spread, 43
English Tea Gingerbread, 48
English Toffee Candy, 159
English Toffee Squares, 81
Espresso Brownies, 65
Fancy Sandwiches, instructions, 26
Finnish Buttermilk Cake, 143
French Nut Drops, 87
Fresh Apple Cake, 141

Fresh Apple Cake Bars, 75
Fresh Ginger Cookies, 125
Friendship Gingersnaps, 120
Fruit Pecan Balls, 161
Fruited Tea Punch, 23
German Pretzel Cookies, 115
German Sand Tarts, 133
Ginger "Tea," 20
Ginger Balls, 162
Ginger Butter Triangles, 33
Ginger Pound Cake, 144
Ginger Rounds, 121
Ginger Spread, 36
Glazed Pecans, 158
Golden Apricot Bars, 75
Golden Lemon Bars, 83
Gougères, 177
Grand Marnier Brownies, 66
Ham Salad Filling, 41
Hazelnut Biscotti with Black Pepper, 172
Hermits, 79
Holiday Lebkuchen, 80
Holiday Nut Cake, 149
Honey Bars, 73
Hundred Dollar Chocolate Cake, 151
Icebox Oatmeal Cookies, 126
Iced Tea, 23
INGREDIENTS AND TECHNIQUES, 8
  Ingredients, 11
  Techniques, 12
Irish Lace Cookies, 104
Irresistible Banana Bread, 51
Jasmine Tea Bread, 47
Javanese Shortbread, 124
Jon Vie Brownies, 65
Lacy Hazelnut Cookies, 105
Ladyfingers, 163
Lavash Sandwiches, instructions, 29
Lemon Curd, 169
Lemon Love Bars, 82
Lemon Nut Cookies, 129
Lemon Tangs, 128
Lemon Thyme Cookies, 129
Lemonade Drops, 91
Linzer Bars, 68
Madeleines, 164
Mayonnaise Spread Sandwiches, 41
Mediterranean Sandwich Wraps, 37
Melted Moments, 101
Michigan Rocks, 100
Mocha Divines, 101
Mocha Rum Balls, 117

Molded Cookies, 108
Mushroom Meringues, 165
Needless Markup Cookies, 96
No Roll Sugar Cookies, 112
Nut Cake, 149
Nut Shortbread, 122
Nut Spread, 36
Nutmeg Cake Squares, 69
Nutmeg Cookie Logs, 117
Nutty Coconut Bars, 70
Oatmeal Crisps, 111
Oatmeal Sugar Cookies, 110
Old Fashioned Oatmeal Cake, 143
Olive Butter, 32
Orange Apricot Cookies, 130
Orange Butter, 35
Orange Cookies, 90
Orange Poppy Seed Cake, 150
Parmesan Palmiers, 175
Peanut Butter Crinkles, 100
Peanut Cookies, 127
Pear and Kiwi Preserve, 162
Pear Bread, 52
Pecan Balls, 114
Pecan Bars, 72
Pecan Cookies, 114
Pecan Turtles, 72
PETITE SANDWICHES AND FILLINGS, 24
  Bacon Filling, 41
  Broccoli Tea Sandwiches, 43
  Butter Spread Sandwiches, 31
  Canapés, instructions, 26
  Carrot Raisin Filling, 43
  Chicken Pecan Sandwiches, 42
  Chicken Salad with Cranberry Chutney, 40
  Chive Butter, 32
  Cinnamon Butter Pinwheels, 33
  Closed Sandwiches, instructions, 27
  Crabmeat Filling, 41
  Cream Cheese Spread Sandwiches, 35
  Cream Cheese and Strawberry Sandwiches, 35
  Cucumber Mint Filling, 43
  Date Bacon Sandwiches, 40
  English Spread, 43
  Fancy Sandwiches, instructions, 26
  Ginger Butter Triangles, 33
  Ginger Spread, 36
  Ham Salad Filling, 41
  Lavash Sandwiches, instructions, 29
  Mayonnaise Spread Sandwiches, 41
  Mediterranean Sandwich Wraps, 37
  Nut Spread, 36

PETITE SANDWICHES AND FILLINGS *(continued)*

Olive Butter, 32

Orange Butter, 35

Pineapple Cheese Wafers, 36

Pinwheel Sandwiches, instructions, 27

Poppy Seed Butter, 32

Raspberry Dainties, 35

Ribbon Sandwiches, instructions, 29

Roasted Red Bell Pepper Canapés, 37

Roquefort Spread, 36

Salmon Dill Rounds, 39

Savory Butter Pinwheels, 32

Shrimp Butter, 31

Smoked Salmon Lavash Sandwiches, 39

Spiced Pear Butter, 33

Spinach Pimiento Roll-ups, 40

Sun-dried Tomato Butter, 31

Tea Sandwiches, instructions, 26

Watercress Butter Roll-ups, 31

Watercress Canapés, 39

Watercress Ham Sandwiches, 42

Pine Nut Cookies, 99

Pine Nut Loaves, 150

Pineapple Cheese Wafers, 36

Pinwheel Sandwiches, instructions, 27

Poppy Seed Butter, 32

POTPOURRI, 156

Caraway Cheese Straws, 176

Chocolate Éclairs, 168

Chocolate Mousse Cups, 171

Chocolate Rum Drops, 162

Chocolate-Dipped Strawberries or Dried Apricots, 167

Cinnamon Nut Palmiers, 173

Cranberry Chutney, 163

Cream Puffs, 169

English Toffee Candy, 159

Fruit Pecan Balls, 161

Ginger Balls, 162

Glazed Pecans, 158

Gougères, 177

Hazelnut Biscotti with Black Pepper, 172

Ladyfingers, 163

Lemon Curd, 169

Madeleines, 164

Mushroom Meringues, 165

Parmesan Palmiers, 175

Pear and Kiwi Preserve, 162

Savory Cheese Wafers, 177

Scottish Shortbread, 176

Simple Delights, 161

Tangy Bourbon Mixed Nuts, 158

Teatime Tassies, 175

Vanilla Caramels, 159

Praline Grahams, 80

Prune Nut Bars, 76

Pumpkin Bars, 78

Pumpkin Bread, 50

Pumpkin Cake Roll, 138

Pumpkin Cookies, 90

Raisin Ginger Cookies, 121

Raspberry Dainties, 35

Refrigerator Bran Muffins, 55

Refrigerator Cookies, 122

Ribbon Sandwiches, instructions, 29

Roasted Red Bell Pepper Canapés, 37

Rolled Cookies, 131

Roquefort Spread, 36

Rosemary Walnut Muffins, 55

Russian Tea, 21

Salmon Dill Rounds, 39

Savory Butter Pinwheels, 32

Savory Cheese Wafers, 177

Scones and Biscuits, 57

Scottish Butter Squares, 81

Scottish Oat Surprises, 88

Scottish Shortbread, 176

Sensational Swedish Slims, 110

Sesame Seed Cookies, 98

SHAPED COOKIES, 106

Almond Slices, 123

Anise Wafers, 122

Apple Cider Cookies, 128

Apricot Balls, 108

Apricot Buttons, 108

Benne Wafers, 112

Brown Sugar Cookies, 112

Buttery Brandy Wreaths, 111

Caraway Crisps, 126

Cardamom Thins, 125

Chocolate Chip Snowballs, 116

Chocolate Crinkles, 116

Christmas Cookies, 109

Cinnamon Roll-ups, 131

Coconut Cookies, 123

Crisp Molasses Cookies, 134

Crispy Pistachio Cookies, 127

Crunchy Pecan Cookies, 114

Dipped Gingersnaps, 119

Fresh Ginger Cookies, 125

Friendship Gingersnaps, 120

German Pretzel Cookies, 115

German Sand Tarts, 133

Ginger Rounds, 121

Icebox Oatmeal Cookies, 126

Javanese Shortbread, 124

Lemon Nut Cookies, 129

Lemon Tangs, 128
Lemon Thyme Cookies, 129
Molded Cookies, 108
Mocha Rum Balls, 117
No Roll Sugar Cookies, 112
Nut Shortbread, 122
Nutmeg Cookie Logs, 117
Oatmeal Crisps, 111
Oatmeal Sugar Cookies, 110
Orange Apricot Cookies, 130
Peanut Cookies, 127
Pecan Balls, 114
Pecan Cookies, 114
Raisin Ginger Cookies, 121
Refrigerator Cookies, 122
Rolled Cookies, 131
Sensational Swedish Slims, 110
Sherry Tumblers, 118
Springerle, 135
Stuffed Monkeys, 119
Sugar Cookies, 133
Sugarless Spice Cookies, 124
Thimble Cookies, 109
Thin Buttery Sugar Cookies, 134
Velvet Spritz Cookies, 118
Whiskey Crescents, 109
White Chocolate and Macadamia Nut Cookies, 115
Sherry Tumblers, 118
Sherry Zucchini Cake, 139
Shrimp Butter, 31
Simple Delights, 161
Sleeping Macaroons, 86
Smoked Salmon Lavash Sandwiches, 39
Snow on the Mountain Bars, 74
Soft Ginger Cookies, 89
Sour Cream Apple Squares, 76
Sour Cream Cookies, 89
Sour Cream Rhubarb Squares, 79
Spiced Apple Bread, 50
Spiced Pear Butter, 33
Spinach Pimiento Roll-ups, 40
Springerle, 135
Stuffed Monkeys, 119
Sugar Cookies, 133
Sugarless Spice Cookies, 124
Sun-dried Tomato Butter, 31
Sunshine Cake, 155
Tangy Bourbon Mixed Nuts, 158
TEA, 14
    Classic Chilled Tea, 22
    Fruited Tea Punch, 23
    Ginger "Tea," 20

Iced Tea, 23
Russian Tea, 21
Tea, the Perfect Pot, 19
Tomato Bouillon "Tea," 21
TEA BREADS, 44
    Apricot Nut Bread, 52
    Blueberry Muffins, 54
    Butterhorns, 61
    Buttermilk Scones, 60
    Cranberry Lemon Bread, 54
    Curry Scones with Chutney Butter, 57
    Date Nut Bread, 48
    English Tea Gingerbread, 48
    Irresistible Banana Bread, 51
    Jasmine Tea Bread, 47
    Pear Bread, 52
    Pumpkin Bread, 50
    Refrigerator Bran Muffins, 55
    Rosemary Walnut Muffins, 55
    Scones and Biscuits, 57
    Spiced Apple Bread, 50
    Tea Lime Bread, 47
    Tiny Tea Biscuits, 58
    Zucchini Bread, 51
Tea Lime Bread, 47
Tea Sandwiches, instructions, 26
Tea, the Perfect Pot, 19
Teatime Tassies, 175
Techniques, 12
Thimble Cookies, 109
Thin Buttery Sugar Cookies, 134
Thin Chocolate Squares, 64
Tiny Tea Biscuits, 58
Toffee Crunch Cookies, 98
Tomato Bouillon "Tea," 21
Tranquility Lemon Cake, 147
Vanilla Caramels, 159
Velvet Spritz Cookies, 118
Vienna Raspberry Chocolate Bars, 68
Walnut Chews, 99
Watercress Butter Roll-ups, 31
Watercress Canapés, 39
Watercress Ham Sandwiches, 42
Whiskey Crescents, 109
White Buttermilk Cake, 154
White Chocolate and Cashew Cookies, 96
White Chocolate and Macadamia Nut Blondies, 69
White Chocolate and Macadamia Nut Cookies, 115
Yogurt Pound Cake, 142
Zebras, 73
Zucchini Bread, 51